TOURISM INDUSTRY
in
India

TOURISM INDUSTRY in

India

TAPAN K. PANDA
SITIKANTHA MISHRA

EXCEL BOOKS

ISBN: 81-7446-338-0

First Edition: New Delhi, 2003

EXCEL BOOKS
A-45, Naraina, Phase I,
New Delhi - 110 028

Published by Anurag Jain for Excel Books, A-45, Naraina, Phase I, New Delhi-110028,
and printed by him at Excel Printers, C-206, Naraina, Phase I, New Delhi - 110 028

CONTENTS

vi

FOREWORD

Effective human resource utilisation shall greatly determine the path of progress for the service industry in the 21st century. This implies a special significance for tourism and travel trade, which primarily revolves around the human factor. Tourism has emerged as a key sector of the world economy and is recognised as the largest industry in the world. It is a catalyst in the development process at national and global levels. Tourism, as an industry, has stimulated employment, investment, strengthened economic structure and made positive contribution to the balance of payments in many developed and developing countries. It has also proved that international harmony fosters national integration and consequently promotes peaceful existence.

The negative growth caused due to series of unfortunate happenings starting from September 11, 2002 attack on World Trade Centre was restricted for the first time in the reported figures for September 2002 where a growth of 9% was reflected. Thereafter monthly arrival figures have been showing consistent increase over the previous years. Hopefully, this trend will continue for a long time to enable us to achieve our targets.

Tourism industry tends to be highly sensitive and vulnerable to external factors. Law and order problems or security threats due to geographic and demographic factors pose to be the biggest enemy of tourism development. Over a period of time, it has been experienced that in every third or fourth year, there has been some untoward incident which adversely affects the growth of tourism in the country. Therefore, in order to develop sustainable tourism, one will have to bear in mind such factors while suggesting a pragmatic strategy.

In India, the government has adopted several measures to draw a more desirable profile for tourism. In view of its immense economic potential, it has been declared a priority area. Accordingly, significant increase in financial allocations, new infrastructure projects at micro level, new integrated tourism circuits, cultural hubs in each state and other initiatives have been taken. There can be no doubt, then, that Indian Tourism is on the ascend. State driven tourism initiatives coupled with private sector enterprise is set to leave no stone unturned to lure the elusive inbound travellers, because domestic tourism will strengthen the base for international tourism. Today, tourism is a far more coordinated product with a far greater emphasis on public-private partnership. It is safe to predict a steady growth in this industry in the future. This is purely a result of new business models, greater awareness, evolving markets, definite indicators of potential growth areas and a host of innovative strategies that will drive this industry into a new era.

It gives me great pleasure to present the book "Tourism Industry in India" edited by Prof Tapan Kumar Panda and .Prof Sitikantha Mishra. Many eminent researchers, planners and academicians have contributed their articles. This book is truly dedicated to expanding the frontiers of knowledge and significantly contribute to the literature on tourism as a social science. In this role, the book both structures and is structured by the research efforts of a multidisciplinary community of scholars. Its premier aim is to publish papers and research work by both practitioners and academics that represent cutting-edge administrative research. I sincerely hope this modest beginning will lead to many more volumes and will stimulate more meaningful research in tourism for sustainable development of tourism in India.

D SINGHAI
Director
IITTM, *Gwalior*

PREFACE

Tourism is the world's biggest industry but India's share of the world tourism market has still remained below half a percent, despite more than half a century of effort. Nature has endowed India with thousands of miles of pristine beaches, lush forests, wildlife, mighty mountains, deserts, a diverse and vibrant culture and many more attractions. Truly India offers, as is often quoted "the world in one place".

Of late, the Government of India has realised the potential of tourism in the generation of employment, foreign exchange and conservation of natural and cultural heritage, in particular and the development of regions, in general. In this context, what the Prime Minister of India observed on Oct 30th, 2001, amply vindicates the changed priority of the Central Government in approaching tourism as an agent of socio-economic change. He said, "tourism is a major engine of economic growth in most parts of the world. It has great capacity to create large scale employment of diverse kinds from the most specialised to the unskilled and all of us know that generation of massive productive employment opportunity is what India needs the most".

In the meantime, the Government has come up with a new tourism policy and conceived many innovative programmes for the 10th Five Year Plan. The budget allocation for the plan period has also been enhanced substantially.

Though the authorities in the country have started giving priorities for the development of international tourism, the domestic tourism segment has still been ignored, perhaps with the assumption that it may not help in generating income and employment. But recent studies have proved that the domestic tourism is a 150 million plus tourist industry contributing about 65 to 70 per cent towards hotel occupancy. It is also interesting to note that more than 100 million Indians travel to different religious places in a year which also is an indication of the importance of pilgrimage tourism in the country.

Further, the growth of outbound tourism has been remarkable in the country which is a strong four million plus market.

Considering the growth potential of the inbound, domestic and outbound tourism market in the country, the policies and the programmes are to be streamlined to meet the requirements of the burgeoning Indian tourism market. A major challenge facing the Indian tourism today is the lack of basic research on tourism and development of trained/qualified professionals to meet the demand of this ever-changing personalised service industry.

Though there are many institutions in the country engaged in the process of creating qualified manpower for tourism, the challenge before the academia is becoming complicated day-by-day because of the change in the tourist activity patterns and preferences.

The book "Tourism Industry in India" is the first in the series of the publications that we plan to bring out through a collaborative effort of tourism scholars, policy makers, researchers as well as practitioners for the sustainable development of tourism in India.

We believe the implementable suggestions/recommendations given by our learned contributors, if acted upon, would definitely prove to be useful for the development of tourism in India.

We are deeply grateful to Shri Devendra Singhai, Director, IITTM, Gwalior, who has kindly agreed to write the foreword for the book.

We are thankful to our wives Julie and Hillolini and kids Tejasvee, Agastya and Amartya for sparing us the time to undertake this work which should have been theirs.

We are grateful to our dear friend, Mr. Anurag Jain (CEO of Excel Books) and Mr. Manish Mullick for their dedicated consideration for bringing out this book within the promised period.

TAPAN KUMAR PANDA
SITIKANTHA MISHRA

SECTION

A

CHAPTER
1

PROSPECTS OF TOURISM INDUSTRY

V M XAVIOUR*

There has been a significant increase in the number of unemployed people in the country during the past years. The figures on the live registers of the employment exchanges have gone up to 38.74 million. Tourism is an ideal sector for the development of the country not only because of the beautiful scenarios but also it would create more jobs. It is an investment friendly sector which has immense growth potential.

Over the past couple of decades, tourism had emerged as an important socioeconomic activity. While on the social side, it promoted international understanding and helped in national integration, on the economic side also it played a significant role. Because of the scope for the enormous foreign exchange earnings and employment generating potential, tourism had emerged as

* Lecturer, Deptt. of Commerce, Management Studies & Tourism and Travel Management, St. Thomas College, Thrissur - 680 001.

the fastest growing industry in the world. Thus, $423 billion global industry with total international arrivals of 592 million tourists offers immense opportunities for every country to share. The world at present has one-tenth of its workforce gainfully employed in tourism sector India has only two per cent of its labour force employed in this sector that has vast potentials for in-house as well as international visitors.

Global trends show that the tourism sector would witness a boom over the next 10 years during which the sector is expected to create 20.94 millions jobs in the Asia Pacific region. In India, the sector provides employment to 80.5 lakh people directly and 120 lakh people indirectly. For every Rs 10 lakhs invested, it creates 47.5 jobs.

Tourism is the third gross foreign exchange earner after gems, jewellery and textiles. India's share in the global tourist arrivals is less than 0.4 per cent while its share in the country's GDP is 1.2 per cent. Even with this tiny global market share, the economic impact of tourism on the country has been significant. In 1997-98 foreign exchange revenue generated from tourism was in excess of Rs 10,000 crores.

South Asia received only 0.8 per cent of world's total tourist arrivals and only one per cent of the total foreign currency generated by tourism globally. According to WTO India was the most favoured destination among countries of the South Asian region receiving more than 50 per cent of the total foreign tourist traffic in the area. India had always beckoned visitors from all over the world to experience its 5000 years old civilisation. The country's diversity of culture, faiths, languages, fairs and festivals, majestic monuments and captivating wildlife made for a variety which could take in almost the whole world. All these provide a unique set of opportunities for tourists to enjoy.

International tourist arrivals to India in 1996-97 were 2.33 million and were expected to be five million by the beginning of the century. It is a pity that a country like Singapore with its population of just about 3 million gets 7 million tourists a year, but India with its population of 1 billion succeeded in tapping only 2.33 million visitors in 1996-97. Tourism is a very crucial and principal sector since many other sectors are vitally linked to its success.

The country will require an investment of about Rs 54.600 Crores to expand its existing tourism infrastructure in terms of airline seats, airports, inland travel, telecommunication and hotel rooms in the next three years. The availability of hotel rooms is very poor in India while China offers 3.9 lakh rooms, Indonesia has 1.68 lakh rooms whereas India can offer only 58,000 rooms. To meet the target of five million tourists by the beginning of the century and growing number of domestic tourists estimated at 100 million today the country requires at least 72,000 additional rooms in the next four years.

Lack of marketing awareness and infrastructure continue to affect the growth of tourism industry. Foreign tourists are also looking for cheaper facilities than five-star hotels. Stress must be made for developing such facilities. Business tourism, conference tourism, shopping tourism, leisure and adventure tourism are high earning categories and India needs to develop this segment.

Travel industry will continue to be good business if professionally run, integrating the latest innovations and technology and understanding the needs of the consumer to deliver quality products and services. There are plans to promote entrepreneurship development as a new dimension to improve tourist services and facilities. Unless we improve our infrastructure and effectively market India we may only be left harping upon our potentials, while others reap the fruits of the industry showing an annual growth of seven per cent the world over.

CHAPTER

2

MAJOR AREAS OF TOURISM AND DEVELOPMENT

Issues & Problems in Unplanned Development of Hill Resorts of Maharashtra

DULARI QURESHI*

My study is mainly based on primary sources. To a large extent my study depends on observation, interviews and mail. I have also used articles from Times of India and the special issue on Maharashtra by Maharashtra Tourism Development Corporation. I have attempted to highlight the specific problems of hill resorts of Maharashtra due to haphazard development on limited land area. Though these hill stations are small and little known compared to the northern or north-eastern hill resorts which are very popular especially with Mumbaites and Puneites.

These charming picturesque hill stations are tucked in the Western Ghats. Most of them belong to the colonial area, when

---

* Professor, Aurangabad University.

the British travelled to escape the intense summer heat of the plains. The majestic mansions and cottages they built integrated aesthetically with highlander environment of these hill stations luxuriant with bush dense forests, waterfalls gurgling from the hills and down the ravines below. Lakes abound here and enhance its fascination for travellers. Some of the more popular hill stations in Maharashtra are Mahabaleshwar. Khandala, Lonavala, Matheran and Panchgani, Mahabaleshwar and Panchgani are famous for their orchid sanctuaries.

Mahabaleshwar and Panchgani are in close proximity. Mahabaleshwar, founded in 1820 by Sir Malcolm, is one of the most beautiful hill stations with several viewpoints named after Britishers. It is also a source of five rivers with important learning on the country's economy. Some of the famous forts of Shivaji Maharaj like Rengarh, Pratapgarh, Sinhagarh are at close quarters. Panchgani is at a stone's throw from Mahabaleshwar and at a slightly lower height. It derives its name from the five hills that surround it. The table and a flat mountain top offer a view of the coastal plains below.

Khandala and Lonavala are the turn resorts on the Mumbai-Pune highway Khandala is specially beautiful during the monsoons as the clouds literally descend on these hills and create a heavenly atmosphere, with dimly visible silvery waterfalls surging down.

The nearest hill station from Mumbai is Matheran and the most frequented. From Victoria Terminus at Mumbai, any Pune bound train will take you up to Neral in about just two hours. From Neral you travel in the most delightful toy train. The Matheran line was constructed in 1907. Earlier a steam engine, is now replaced by diesel locomotives, which is a pleasurable journey. The route is noted for its unbelievable curves and the forest sharp curve is marketed by a large notice, which says, Dopes, What a curve! 45 feet radius. The best part of Matheran is its complete freedom from petrol fumes and the cacophony of cars and buses as the only access to the hill is the toy train. A real treat to the crowded public after the noise, congestion and polluting air of Mumbai.

The sylvan, original splendour of these hill stations is unfortunately in an appalling condition now. The earlier pure crisp mountain air, untouched virgin beauty of the dense forests, waterfalls, literal paradises nestling in the Sahyadri hills are presently besieged by multiple polluting problems.

As tourism is booming we witness a staggering increase from a few thousands to lakhs of arrivals, thanks to the several travel agents offering attractive packages. Even the rainy season, which always was sluggish, presently is the most attractive season to visit these hill stations. Packages like bonus days, free travel and designer holidays are a successful pull. Concept of home away from home, time-share concept modified into membership scheme are all seducing the moneyed Mumbaites to greet the rains.

According to the membership scheme, a member who deposits Rs 56,000, at the end of twelve years gets Rs 90,000. During his membership period he himself and his four guests can spend a week at resorts in Matheran, Mahabaleshwar or Manali or at 20 other hotels with which the travel agency has a tie-up. While the deposit money takes care of the stay, members are entitled to a 20% food discount. These are two other membership categories, casual and off-seasons, for which the deposits are Rs 34,000 and Rs 20,000 respectively. All these packages have removed the earlier 'Off – season' and replaced it with season all round the year. The results are profits that are sky-high and resorts are raking in the moolah.

The hills are teaming with tourists, crowding the microscopic hill stations, unconsciously causing severe strain on these natural splendorous.

ISSUES AND PROBLEMS

One of the major issues tormenting these beautiful hills is the emergence of builders, who have increasingly commercialised the resorts. There has been a construction boom and new hotels are cropping up each day.

These new hotels are mostly two or three storeyed buildings which are causing grave architectural pollution. Large dominating hotel buildings are often out of scale and clash with the lush green surroundings of the mountains. The large structures inevitably stick out of the woods giving it an ugly look. Several colonial cottages and mansions which balanced perfectly with the environment are being rampantly demolished. The red earth gardens and driveways too are being replaced by cement concrete. Uncouth, flashy buildings are scarring the scenic vista.

Secondly, the increase in construction activity is causing water shortage due to the increased water demand for construction. Locals from Matheran are facing acute water shortage. The grouse of the inhabitants is against the swimming pools in big hotels, water sports where water available is plenty, whereas the locals face the water shortage problem.

Another reason for water shortage is low voltage during summers. This means that the pumps, which provide water to the resorts 100 metres above peak, cause overflow of waste water rousing not only stench but contaminating local waterfalls and ground water system and gradually the rivers and reservoirs in the area.

Due to increase in the tourist number, the gardens, viewpoints, lake sides have witnessed a growth of unauthorised eating stalls. The stalls not only pollute the various scenic beauty spots by dumping garbage but also scar the beauty of these lakes and gardens. The horse rides at the lake side add to the mess, as their dung and urine flow into the lake. Garbage has been piling up in all hill stations. This excessive dumping of garbage is not only ugly but can also change the nutrient status of soils and can be ecologically damaging by blocking out air and light.

Much of the attraction of hill stations lies not so much in the natural panoramic scenes as the absence of humans for which the tourists travel to hill resorts. But the crowds pouring on roads, gardens, viewpoints disenchant the tourist and frustrate them.

Traffic congestion has emerged as one of the more serious consequences of resort development. Parking space demand is increasing. Thus, the hill resorts of Maharashtra are becoming overdeveloped with high-rise buildings, afforestation, water shortage, noise and pollution and high prices. Antagonism of the locals is on the increase as the tourist enjoys special facilities and the locals are suffering from daily problems.

One of the cardinal reasons pointed out for this agonising state of the hill resorts of Maharashtra is the low priority policy of the State Government given to tourism. In fact, though most of these resorts are thriving, the state government, has not put in any effort to develop them since last 50 years. A few new hills stations are coming up, but the state government does not play any role in their development and is inviting private sector to develop new hill stations. Others reasons pointed out are the lack of manpower technical aids and up-to-date maps of the region.

Suggestions

To arrest the hazards of rampant pollution, the civic authorities should immediately chalk out an action plan.

(1) First of all, a survey of the problem area in all the hill stations should be conducted.

(2) Steps should be taken to protect and conserve the forest cover without which the tourists will not be attracted.

(3) New laws should be framed for its sustainable development.

(4) Ministry of Environment should ban any further tree cutting. Laws should be enacted against deforestation and any such attempt should be severely punished.

(5) Awareness campaigns should be conducted in all schools, the locals should also be educated to protect the environment. Ecology slide shows, films should be shown.

(6) The civic authorities should be given more power to make their own urgent decisions.

(7) Most of these hill stations should be declared Eco-Fragile.

(8) Unauthorised stalls should not be allowed to grow near lakes and gardens. Garbage disposal bins should be kept near the stalls, tourists should be instructed to throw the garbage in the bins.

(9) All heavy vehicles should be parked at the entry point and not allowed in the interiors.

(10) Modern sewerage system should be built and better civic amenities provided.

(11) A special workshop for builders and hoteliers should be conducted by the tourism department.

(12) Influx of tourists should be discouraged to some extent.

If all these or at least some of these suggestions are incorporated, the sylvan charm of the hill stations will not be destroyed. Though presently several committees for conservation of these hill stations have been constituted by the state government, more efforts are necessary. Last term plans should be laid down and systematic development should only be allowed.

CHAPTER
3

REFORMS IN TOURISM SECTOR: ECONOMIC AND RESOURCE ISSUES

FANI BHUSAN DAS*

Tourism policy reform is defined as change action or procedure in conformity to judicious provisions of tourism products and services from natural, cultural and man-made resources contributing to economic and social productive activities within the framework of national accounts and ethos. Conceptualisation of reforms is to be considered in relation to status of the society at a particular point of time, future aspirations, directions of growth and capacity to accept change. It is essential to have continuity of policy to ensure uniformity in the pattern of developmental changes for a length of time. This will have positive effect on maximisation of intra and inter generational benefits. Short-term

* Consultant "Bioncureharmentes Technology", Former Commissioner-Secretary of Government of Orissa and Administrator, Indian Institute of Tourism & Travel Management, Ministry of Tourism, Govt. of India, Bhubaneswar.

policies do not yield sustainable impacts in time and space. Policies derived from multiple number of Acts lack comprehension and lead to confusion, adversely affecting growth. Sustainable policies can be formulated with legislative support and framework structured exclusively for a sector like tourism – a multi disciplinary sector with elements of nature, socioeconomic culture, psychology, emotion and technology.

This paper does not intent to deal with legislation aspect of tourism. It provides some of the critical guidelines for formulation of sustainable tourism policies, the reasons for such mindset are (a) it is one of the pillars for promoting country's domestic, economic and foreign exchange growth (b) it is highly labour intensive (c) it helps in poverty alleviation (d) it protects environment and promotes its conservation (e) it provides synergy in cultural assimilation (f) it provides support to local community. But the future role of tourism is more challenging. With accelerated changes taking place throughout the globe, there will be emergence of a new role of tourism as an "experience maker" which will be very crucial for the man to cope with changes. The future of man's organisation is techno-transient society where there will be higher turnover of relationships with places, goods and members of the society. Rapid changes in human institutions of society, family and other organisations will give rise to urgent necessity of shaping social experiences and individual psychology to maintain and improve quality of life. Tourism as an experience maker has the potential to provide psychic-gratification to restless members of the human society in addition, it can reduce stress and bring about a balance between "thought" and "feeling" (improving quality of human species?) which will enable man to think and act with wisdom to achieve sustainability of meaningful changes. Experience industry is emerging, which is the next stage to service industry. Tourism will be one of the vital sectors in guiding and strengthening the experience industry. Whole contributions will meet the future needs of transient technosociety. It is now, therefore, the right time to formulate sustainable tourism reform policies to remove present barriers of growth, and to take care of the future.

Resource is fundamental without which nothing in the world would have been created. Products are made from resources for consumption purpose. Services help to consume products. Resource-Product-Service processes constitute economic productive activities. Central aspects of tourism are also Resource-Product-Service to which travel, transportation, accommodation, infrastructure (physical, social, and economic), hospitality, human resource development, marketing and business, etc., are linked. Tourism resources are broadly divided into three types, viz. nature, culture and man-made, from which products like destinations, attraction, etc. are manufactured and the services help to consume such products. There is now urgent need for formulation of Basic Tourism Reform Policy (BTRP). This deals with central aspects to tourism, i.e. the Resource-Product-Service and its linkages to understanding of economic priorities.

ECONOMIC DIMENSION OF TOURISM

First, it is necessary to make travel and tourism an economic activity and its incorporation in the framework of national accounts. It depends on local resources, supports local community and has a high percentage of foreign exchange retention. It generates both direct and indirect jobs. During 1997, about 262 million people constituting 10.5% of global workforce were employed in this sector, which will grow to 383 million in 2007, which means one new job will be created every 2.4 seconds. It has also the potential to be a key element in the national strategy to improve foreign exchange, boost exports, and encourage investment. It has direct and indirect effect in creating GDP, increasing tax revenue and appreciating jobs contributing substantially to the growth of economy with proactive policy framework.

Policy makers should realise the importance of tourism in the economy. Some of the logical determinants of this view are briefly dealt within the following paragraphs.

Tourism is "demand" concept for which tourism consumption leads to "purchase" although it generates some difficult adjustment in the aggregates of demand. Consumption can be divided into four groups, viz. (A) Domestic tourism consumption (B) Inbound tourism consumption (C) International tourism consumption (D) Outbound tourism consumption. This constitutes "total tourism consumption" as an interacting aggregate, which would indicate size of tourism as compared to total goods and services and economic output from the resources developed. It can be compared to GNP or GDP in the same way as total import, total household final consumption or the deficit of public sector. However, it will be difficult to express it as share of GNP/GDP.

"Supply" concept focuses on the economic productive activities, which are in close interface with the tourists. The economic importance of this activity is "value added" and characterises economic productivity ar..d measures the additional values created by the production process. This can be expressed by the equation VA (value added) = OV (output value) – VIC (value of intermediate consumption used up in the productive process). Value added can be compiled from establishments whose principal activity consists in delivering goods and services to the tourists exclusively.

In addition to above, open and competitive markets should be developed within the overall global trading framework. Infrastructure especially air transport system is vital to economic growth. The principles of sustainable development should be pursued, which will increase the contribution of tourism sector to the national economy. Steps may also be taken to eliminate barriers to growth so that the industry can be developed to provide genuine long-term demand, drive sustainable growth, foreign exchange, jobs and cultural integration.

The interface between tourism and public economics and environmental economics should be understood. Government invests in infrastructure required for tourism, which raises the issue of financing its supply. Bed taxes, levies on hotel account, user's charges of tourism products/services, high visa charges, airport taxes, etc. can be imposed on tourists. Government revenue can be augmented directly by the tourists via values added taxes (VAT). Besides, with increase in tourism incomes in the companies/organisations, taxes can be collected on the basis of rate of increase of incomes and revenues. Imposition of taxes by the government will have to take into account the economic factors such as elasticity of demand of visits to the destinations and tourist visits because this will affect public revenue from such changes. When market failure occurs, government involvement in economic allocation may be necessary, provided benefits of intervention outweigh the costs involved.

Charging tourists for use of natural environments and "polluter to pay" principles can also be adopted for providing gratification and to repair the damages caused to the environmental assets.

Tourism economics calls for interdisciplinary understanding and approach. Effective strategy can be adopted to ensure greater share of this growth. In next few decades of human development, there is every possibility that "Experience Industry" will appear as a major revolution, of which tourism will play a very crucial role. It is therefore, now necessary to initiate proactive measures and research to determine the role and impact of "experience industry development" economics in the national economy.

With right economic reform policy implemented, tourism resource development reform can be conceptualised for fostering social and economic benefits with clear long-term goals and objectives. Objective, dictate policy formulation. An attempt has been made in the following paragraphs to identify objective and policies for the central aspects of tourism, i.e. Resource – Products – Services.

Tourism Resources

(i) **Natural Resources**

    (a) *Objectives*

        (i) Flora and Fauna to be fully protected;

        (ii) Prevention of destruction of wildlife habitat;

        (iii) Preservation of natural resources and facilitate preservation with architectural and landscape designs reflecting local traditions;

        (iv) Safeguard and strengthen host community's quality of life with innovations like, developing economic products from nature which can also act as tourist products;

        (v) Maintenance of ecological balance.

    (b) *Policies*

        (i) Scientific methodology to study and identify resources by use of remote sensing maps;

        (ii) Services, buffer and core areas of resources to be integrated, specifying the role of each;

        (iii) Resource development to provide psychic-gratification;

        (iv) Development of infrastructure and services in conformity with spirit and tranquility of resources;

(v) Pollutionless transport modes to be innovated to maintain peace in nature;

(vi) Security of species and their habitats to be ensured by meticulous planning of tourist circuits;

(vii) Tourist flow to be regulated within the carrying capacity of resources;

(viii) Adverse impact on resources to be minimised by innovating eco-friendly carrying materials for tourist, providing opportunity for local entrepreneurship development in the area;

(ix) Service System of Nature (SSN) to be promoted for pollution free development and to innovate economic products from tourism resources;

(x) Architectural and landscaping design standards to be evolved to reinforce the base of natural resources.

Natural resources being very sensitive, it should be ensured that there is convergence of "ecology" and "ethics" through consensus and coalition while exploring the resources for tourism, so that we can really be optimistic about our future.

(ii) Cultural Resources

(a) *Objective*

(i) Strengthening of intra and inter-cultural goodwill, fostering understanding relationships;

(ii) Minimisation of cross-cultural adverse impacts;

(iii) Preservation of monuments, historic sites and places;

(iv) Strengthening of traditional cultural patterns, arts, architecture, handicrafts, music, dance, folklores and maintenance of the essence of beliefs and practices.

(b) *Policies*

   (i) Social learning process from cultural- resources to be recognised and promoted;

   (ii) Socio-cultural patterns to be studied and analysed to design programmes to improve and strengthen relationship of guest and host communities;

   (iii) Impact assessment study on culture to be made and measures to be initiated before the destinations are opened to foreign groups;

   (iv) Concept of sensitising tourists to be developed to regulate their behaviour;

   (v) Essence of culture to be properly marketed through different channels of expression and communication;

   (vi) Regulatory guidelines to be developed for maintenance of spirit of monuments and historic sites and places;

   (vii) Revitalising and promoting art, handicrafts, music, dance, etc.

Product Development

(a) *Objectives*

   (i) Tourism products to be an integrated part of general development programme;

   (ii) Products to satisfy inner urge of gratification;

(iii) To stimulate economic development and redistribution of income directed more towards less development zones;

(iv) Product development to be in conformity with environmental and socio-cultural harmony;

(v) Interface of products and tourists to promote mutual support and understanding in the society.

(b) *Policies*

(i) Exploration process of destinations and attractions through holistic approach and within economic, social, environmental and cultural framework;

(ii) Continuous evaluation of product performance for assessment of environmental quality and socio-cultural impacts;

(iii) The general planning process both at macro and micro level to identify tourism products and make provisions for overall development;

(iv) Product development organisation and management structure to be organically designed;

(v) Measures to be planned for sustainability of products;

(vi) Product development to be linked to provision of supporting facilities, services and infrastructure.

Service Development

(a) *Objectives*

(i) Continuous improvement of quality of service development;

(ii) Integrated service packages of tour and travel, accommodation and other facilities to be promoted;

(iii) Tourist satisfaction to be maximised;

(iv) Changing tourist needs to be met;

(v) Easy access to tourism information service with accuracy to be provided.

(b) *Policies*

(i) Service organisations to be professionalised to deliver goods matching tourist expectation;

(ii) Information technology services should be promoted to make it an inseparable unit or service organisation;

(iii) Capacity building of various organisations providing services, to be taken up on continuous basis;

(iv) Effective control and supervision system to be designed on the quality level of hospitality, food and drink along with level of hygiene;

(v) Formulation of appropriate fiscal policies to enable service providers to improve quality;

(vi) Service development strategy to be formulated to increase marketability of products;

(vii) Delivery of intangible aspects like emotion, gratification, etc., to be given priority by incorporating suitable elements in service delivery systems.

The objectives and reform policies spelled out for strengthening the cutting edge of tourism management are not exhaustive. Such a framework for development of resources, products and services is the foundation for further development of a proactive tourism reform policy. There is an urgent need of such policy formulation which will ensure sustainable tourism development in the country, maximising overall economic, social cultural and ecological advantage of tourism while respecting the dynamics of balanced tourism supply and demand.

SOCIO POLITICAL BARRIER TO TOURISM MARKETING IN SOUTH ASIA

SITIKANTHA MISHRA*
TAPAN K PANDA**

Tourism is a smokeless industry and is one of the fast growing businesses world over. The tourist flow to various countries serves as an indicator through which we can foresee a process of cultural assimilation and economic development in destination countries. Every country has something to offer to a tourist, it may be in the form of natural products like scenic spots or man-made wonders like Disneyland in USA. Many of the developing countries are blessed with such a vast amount of cultural heritage, material artifacts and lifestyles embedded with fairs and festivals that tourism industry can serve as a great source of revenue generation. Despite

* Professor and Administrator, Indian Institute of Travel and Tourism Management, Bhubaneswar.
** Faculty Member, Indian Institute of Management, Lucknow.

the nature's gift in abundance in countries and particularly in South Asia, the tourist traffic has remained dismally low and the region receives a minute percentile of the global traffic. This paper is an attempt to find out the reasons of this poor response world over and identify the perceived barriers or risks. The paper identifies two kinds of sociopolitical barriers like regionalised socio political risk and global sociopolitical risk responsible for poor traffic in the South Asian region. The paper also highlights various other perceived risks like health issues, economic issues and image issues found to be responsible for poor traffic flow to the area.

Key Words – *Tourism, Sociopolitical risk, terrorism, image issues, health issues and economic issues.*

INTRODUCTION

Tourism is the second largest growing business area after information technology in the global economy. Many of the economies are successful in marketing their country as destinations and generating a substantial amount of foreign exchange from tourism sector. Even countries with poor level of infrastructure and facilities are able to attract investors to invest money in their country for tourism promotion.

Tourism promotion, like other forms of marketing, largely depends on the customer traffic. If there is a growing customer traffic trend then more and more money shall flow to an economy in the form of gross revenue earnings and also as foreign direct investments for tourism destination marketing. The product marketing does not involve much complexity like tourism marketing. Tourism marketing is a very complex phenomenon because the number of uncontrollable factors is more than the number of marketing mix variables. Though the conventional marketing wisdom says that larger social and political factors affect the marketing offer in product marketing but it is more prominent in the case of tourism marketing.

The political upspring, terrorism, religious fundamentalism, level of crime perception by the foreign tourist affect the prospects of a destination. The South Asian nations are facing a downturn in the tourism business due to the above reasons. The factors of low per capita tourist investment sustained effort for tourism marketing by the developing countries have become secondary today. The tourism business is largely governed by the non-marketing factors than pure business propositions in South Asia. The geo-political developments and the kind of social background have largely affected the perception of the foreign tourists negatively for which the inbound traffic is in a downturn.

The decision to establish or maintain a direct investment position abroad necessitates addressing the issue of risk that confronts multinational firms. In the examination of any foreign direct or indirect investment opportunity, the environment encompasses numerous areas of concern for the investing firm. One of the main functions of risk analysis is to determine when and how economic and non-economic factors can affect the foreign investment climate in a particular country, given that risk is a direct outcome of the political and non-political realities faced by international business.

Furthermore, this activity is even more crucial in the current global market-place, given the increasingly complex and uncertain environmental conditions faced by international tourism promoters, particularly to developing countries.

SOCIO POLITICAL RISK

The business literature speaks about socio political risk in many ways. For example, Weston and Sorge have pointed that risk arising from actions of governments or political forces which interfere with or prevent foreign business transactions, or change the terms of agreements, or cause the confiscation of wholly or partially foreign owned business property are called socio political risks.

These arise from the uncertainty of social and political events that affect business, rather than with the events themselves. Friedmann and Kim define it as business risk brought by non-economic and broad social factors to the business. A socio political risk event is any outcome in the host country which if it occurs, would have a negative impact on the success of the venture and investment flow. So we can summarise the socio political risk as foreign investors' risk or probability of occurrence of some social and political event(s) that will negatively change the prospect for the profitability of a given investment in the host country.

SOCIO POLITICAL RISK AND TOURISM PROMOTION

Socio political risk always plays a negative role to reduce the availability of factors and opportunities of tourism promotion. Investment in destination promotion, infrastructure development to connect the destination, accommodation facilities, food service, transportation services and retail investments will be discouraged as the risk of capital loss will tend to rise, primarily because social, political and economic rules governing investments are likely to fluctuate, thereby increasing the uncertainty in the future net return associated with investment projects. Such increased risks would also raise the cost of capital, as the likelihood of loan defaults would go high and the period of completion of various projects would also rise. Both domestic and international inbound tourism would be discouraged due to such risks. Indeed, capital flight and leakage might be additional outcomes as well.

As socio political risk introduces additional elements of uncertainty into the rules governing tourism investment projects, the risk of capital loss is raised for longer term projects. Hence, overall productivity in an economy is likely to be lowered via a shift in the marginal efficiency of investment schedule.

Socio political risk also negatively influences the timing and pricing of the tourism production process. For example, the tourism destination planned and promoted with an expected period of launching will not work due to delay in the process of completion of the facilities. So the huge capital invested by intermediaries in promoting destinations in international market will go haywire due to this problem. The traffic planning of the airlines will also be largely affected by this process. Tourism marketing is a circuitry exercise where multiple sectors are dependent on each other. In a combination, they build up a whole tourism product.

The increased expectations of changes and uncertainties in the rules of operation of airlines diminish reliability, but they would also produce erratic stops and starts in other tourism investment projects. The economy as a whole would, therefore, experience a lack of optimal growth path. Thus, it can be argued that political risks increase the uncertainty of the environment in which successful foreign tourism promotion should take place, and hence decrease the incentive to save and invest in tourism by an individual tourist to a particular country destination.

TRAVEL INTERMEDIARIES AND TOURISM PROMOTION

Travel intermediaries are defined as members in the distribution chain in the tourism marketing channel. They include retail travel agents, tour packagers, incentive marketers, tour wholesalers. They provide lodging, transportation and other travel products and services demanded by domestic and foreign tourists. The ability of travel intermediaries to combine travel products and offer them to customers as a package at a price generally lower than those available to individuals, provides travel economy and convenience for a significant segment of tourists.

Travel intermediaries have considerable influence in the decision making process of the tourist. They serve as an opinion leader and expert for taking a travel decision process. They play the role of influencers for many of their loyal customers. This implies that they are of great importance to both the tourist and the destination marketer particularly in cases of destinations with far greater distance from the point of origin. McLellan and Noe identified them as gatekeepers of information, since they provide information about destinations even if travellers do not choose to use their services. Hawkins and Hudman are of the opinion that the distribution sector of tourism is much stronger and travel intermediaries have far greater power to influence and affect tourist demand when compared to their counterparts in other industries.

THE PROBLEM

Despite its variety and immense tourism potential, South Asia's share of the total global tourist arrivals and revenue receipts is meagre. This small proportion is concentrated in a few countries particularly India, Nepal and a few parts of Srilanka. One of the most important factors responsible for this poor growth is the phenomenon of socio political risk events. Since tourism is an extremely fragile industry, a crucial consideration in a potential traveller's decision to visit a foreign destination is regarding the country's political stability, social coherence and other real or perceived barriers like service quality, poor infrastructure and health issues.

Given the spate of socio political risk events in many counties in South-Asia since the late 1980s, little published research in the tourism literature to date has addressed this problem in any comprehensive manner. The purpose of the study is to examine the effects of touristic attractiveness, channel power and socio political risk on the performance of tourism promotion firms and on travel intermediaries. The two broad purposes of this study are to assess empirically the perceived impact of selected socio political risk variables and to identify other perceived environmental barriers and threats to tourism promotion in South Asia.

REVIEW OF LITERATURE

In the tourism literature, few researchers have examined the issue of political risk in South Asian countries and its effects on tourism promotion. Authors have cited socio political risk, lack of investment capital and distance from major tourist generating markets as barriers to tourism promotion in South Asia in general. Negative images, lack of foreign exchange for tourism development, lack of skilled manpower, weak institutional framework for tourism planning, political instability caused by communal violence, civil war conflicts are inhibitors to tourism development. However, little is known about how international tourism firms perceive socio political risks and other general barriers and threats to tourism promotion in South Asia.

As stated above, the major source of knowledge upon which this research has been drawn, for the delineation of socio political risk factors for tourism, is from socio political risk variables existing in general business. The general business literature describes social political risk with illustrations such as civil war, labour conflict, foreign exchange control, production quotas and import-export restrictions. Simon's typology is used for this study.

TABLE 1: MAJOR SOCIO POLITICAL RISK VARIABLES SELECTED FOR THE STUDY

▶   Revolution
▶   Civil war
▶   Factional conflict
▶   Ethnic violence
▶   Religious turmoil

Contd...

- ▶ Widespread riots
- ▶ Terrorism
- ▶ Nationwide strikes/ protests/ boycotts
- ▶ Cross national guerrilla warfare
- ▶ World public opinion
- ▶ Repatriation restrictions
- ▶ Leadership struggle
- ▶ High inflation
- ▶ Bureaucratic politics
- ▶ Border conflicts
- ▶ High external debt service ratio
- ▶ Creeping nationalisation

Source: Simon (1982)

In analysing the impact of socio political risk events on less-developed countries (LDCs), Richter suggests three reasons that may have negative impacts on tourism. For developing nations, instability in a region may negatively affect neighbouring nations due to interruption of air, sea or overland routes and also publicity about instability makes the whole region appear volatile. Internal upheaval within a country may be far from tourist areas or close enough to spill over into areas frequented by tourists. Sometimes foreign tourists are deliberately targeted by anti-government forces to embarrass the government, weaken it economically, and draw international attention abroad to the political conditions in the country.

Richter is of the opinion that such events are highlighted further by western media, who very often force disasters, communal violence and revolutionary activities into the headlines. One of the most common problems of socio political instability and tourism is that episodic violence or conflict far removed from tourist areas receives so much media attention that it appears the entire nation is engulfed in violence. Thus in tourism marketing, perceptions of insecurity by potential travellers is a more significant deterring variable for a destination marketer compared to the level of real socio political problems in the country.

METHODOLOGY

A questionnaire was designed by taking the socio political risk variables explained in Table 1, to measure the effect of socio political risk on a tourism firm's profitability. A five point scale with 5 as the most significant negative effect and 1 as very insignificant negative effect was used. The respondents were asked to list different kinds of barriers and threats perceived by them as concern factors in doing business in their respective South Asian destinations through a series of open ended questions in the designed instrument. An attempt was made to gain insights into both the qualitative and quantitative aspects of the travel intermediaries' perceptions.

Sampling Procedure and Data Collection

Data for this study was collected between October 2000 and January 2001 which happens to be the main tourist season in various parts of South Asia. Members of Indian Association of Tour Operators (IATO) and Indian Association of Travel Agents (IATA) were contacted to supplement the research with a list of clientele of international travel intermediaries operating from various European nations and American states for the survey. These organisations were selected because they provided a membership listing of firms that can be consistently and practically identified as tour operators, destination marketing firms and travel agents whose revenues are derived from packaging and selling tours to South Asian countries.

A sample for the study was drawn using the proportional stratified systematic random sampling method. The sample size was determined to be 230. Of the 230 questionnaires mailed, 27 had undeliverable addresses. After a follow-up, 169 questionnaires were returned, with 129 usable, representing a response rate of

28.6 per cent. Although low, such a response rate is typical of mail questionnaire studies that involve business enterprises, in contrast to survey research that involves individuals. The business owners and managers of the organisations selected for the study often face severe time constraints as a result of their work activities and are often inundated with paperwork, meetings and travel making the process to go slow as per their convenience.

DATA ANALYSIS

Descriptive statistics were calculated for all variables comprising the scaled socio political risk variables. Factor analysis through principal component analysis of the seventeen risk variables was conducted to examine the relationship among the interrelated variables. This procedure resulted in two factors. Only factors with eigen values greater than 1.0 were included in the final analysis. The extracted factors were rotated using the varimax orthogonal rotation method. A variable was considered to load on a given factor if the factor loading was 0.40 or greater for that factor and less than 0.4 for the other. The reliability of the factors was determined using Cronbach's coefficient alpha test.

The main criterion for inclusion in a particular region is if a respondent indicated sending at least two states or districts in a country then he is included in the region. Those who indicated at least two countries in South Asian region, they were classified into the multiple region categories. This is done due to the possibility of within country variability in responses to the perceived risk for a country due to the travel intermediary's business link with that country for promoting tourism. The researcher also tried to investigate the relationships between the underlying socio political risk factors and respondents' particular country of tourism promotion in South Asia. Perception towards socio political barriers and threats to tourism promotion is obtained using an open ended format of the survey instrument.

The researcher conducted content analysis for all open ended questions in which groupings were made for similar responses into categories and assigning names to the common correlated elements. Content analysis is a research method that uses a set of procedures to make valid inferences from text. The central idea is that many of the words of the text are classified into content categories. Words, phrases or other units of text classified in the same category are presumed to have similar meanings. This similarity may be based on the precise meaning of the word, or on words sharing similar connotations. This paper has adopted a similar procedure to group several words implying a concern with concept of perceived barriers and threats in South Asia in an attempt to make valid inferences from the open ended responses.

RESULTS AND DISCUSSIONS

Respondents' Profile

The characteristics of the firms are presented in Table 2. Tour operators constituted the largest proportion of respondents (46.5 per cent), while travel agents and others (airlines, hotels and destination marketing organisations) constituted 35.6 per cent and 17.8 per cent respectively.

TABLE 2: BUSINESS CLASSIFICATION OF RESPONDENTS

Firm characteristics	N	Percentage
Tour operator	60	46.5
Travel agent	46	35.7
Other	23	17.8

Size of the Firm

Most responding firms are small. Over 48 per cent with annual sales of less than Rs 250,000; 25.8 per cent had sales between Rs 250,000 and Rs 749,000; 10.9 per cent ranged in sales from Rs 750,000 to Rs 1.7m; 8.5 percent had sales of between Rs 1.7m and Rs 3.4m, while 4.9 per cent sold over Rs 3.5 million worth of business. Since a typical tour package can range in cost from Rs 25000 to 90,000, one must be careful not to consider sales volume in isolation, since there may not be a direct correlation between gross annual sales and passengers carried.

TABLE 3: GROSS SALES

Gross Sales (Rs)	Frequency	Percentage
Less than 249,999	67	52.0
250,000 – 749,999	31	24.3
750,000 – 1,749m	14	10.9
1.75m – 3.4m	11	8.5
3.5 m or over	6	4.9

Tenure of Business

The number of years that the respondents have been doing business in South Asia is also presented in the following table. It indicates that the majority of respondents, 65.9 per cent (n=83) fall into the category of those that have been in the South Asian tour market since the 1980s, while 31.1 per cent (n =43) constitute those who stared before 1980.

TABLE 4: LIFE OF BUSINESS

Length of time of business Promotion to South Asia		
before 1980	46	35.6
Between 1980 and 1994	83	64.3

MOST FREQUENTLY MENTIONED DESTINATION

The respondents were asked about the destinations which are most frequented by the tourists. This was a top of the mind unaided recall. The respondents are following both push and pull model for marketing the destinations. Some of the destinations are very popular among the tourists and they automatically search for information about these destinations whereas some of the travel intermediaries promote various destinations as a part of circuit promotion. These destinations are pushed through the loyal customers. The intermediaries take more proactive strategy for promoting these destinations. The direct benefit out of this strategy is the longer duration of stay of the tourist in the destination country which leads to more spending and the cost of the package goes high.

On the secondary front, the tourists' risk perception also goes down when they choose an extended stay in a country. In a normal traditional circuit, the tourists follow a short and fast paced circuit and come out of the country. Though this is a conventional method of travelling all over the world but the per capita expenditure of the tourist remains stagnant due to fast pace of travelling and shorter stay. In contrast to this when a destination is promoted for a longer duration, the direct benefit goes to the hospitality sector like hotel, airlines, facilitating organisations and the indirect benefit goes to the secondary economy where the tourist spends an amount on local purchases and local entertainment. The respondents identified following destinations as the most preferred due to higher tourist traffic and higher earnings.

TABLE 5: RANKING OF TEN MOST FREQUENTLY MENTIONED DESTINATIONS IN SOUTH ASIA

Destination	Frequency	Percentages	Rank
Taj Mahal	64	10.8	1
Jaipur	60	10.2	2
New Delhi	41	6.9	3
Colombo	38	6.4	4
Maldives	38	6.4	4
Kathamandu	35	5.9	6
Ajanta/Ellora	33	5.6	7
Islamabad	31	5.3	8
Goa	30	5.1	9
Kandy	20	3.4	10
Dhaka	20	3.4	10
Mumbai	20	3.4	10
Anuradhapuram	20	3.4	10

The majority of respondents perceived terrorism, civil wars, widespread cross-cultural riots and guerrilla warfare as contributing the most negative effect on their profits with a high mean scores (4.3). Although these figures may appear high, the standard deviations of the more direct and externally related factors like negative world public opinion, strong nationalistic movement, profit repatriation restrictions, inflation, high external debt service ratio and the perception regarding socio political risk factors appear to be a better reflection of respondent's opinions of the impact of socio political risk events on profits.

They indicate that even though internal socio political risk events in South Asia may have negative impacts on international tourism channel intermediaries, they may still be able to operate and be profitable due to their internal nature. However, externally related events may have deeper implications for investments and profits. This may be due to the fact that potential tourists may be less likely to book tours since they are more likely to be aware of such events through their local and national media as well as other external sources.

TABLE 6: RESPONDENTS' PERCEPTIONS REGARDING THE EFFECTS OF POLITICAL RISK EVENTS ON PROFIT PROBABILITIES IN SOUTH ASIA

Item	Mean score	Standard deviation	Rank
Terrorism	4.3	0.961	1
Civil wars	4.3	0.918	1
Cross-cultural riots	4.3	1.02	1
Guerrilla warfare	4.3	0.957	1
Ethnic/ Religious turmoil	4.2	0.964	2
Political revolution	4.2	0.974	2
Factional conflicts	4.1	0.922	3
Nationwide strikes, protests/boycotts	4.0	1.08	4
Border conflicts	4.0	1.05	4
Negative world public opinion	3.8	1.20	5
Strong nationalisation	3.7	1.18	6
Profit expatriation restrictions	3.7	1.20	6
Political leadership struggles	3.7	1.23	6
Bureaucratic politics	3.7	1.20	6
High inflation rates	3.4	1.34	8
High debt service ratio	3.4	1.34	8
Bureaucratic politics	3.4	1.34	8

Note: Respondents were asked to respond on a five-point Likert scale to indicate their degree of agreement or disagreement with respect to selected items as per the following

1 = very insignificant effect; 2 = somewhat insignificant effect; 3 = neutral effect; 4 = somewhat significant effect; 5 = very significant effect.

RESULTS OF FACTOR ANALYSIS FOR GROUPING VARIABLES

Results of the factor analysis revealed two factors: regionalised socio political risk, and globalised socio political risk. The factor loadings were found to be high and the two factors accounted for 69.3 per cent of the total variance, with very high Cronbach's reliability coefficients of 0.915 and 0.892 respectively.

TABLE 7: FACTOR ANALYSIS OF SOCIO POLITICAL RISK VARIABLES IN SOUTH ASIA

Factor	Factor Loading	Eigen value	Percentage variance	Reliability coefficient
A. Regionalised socio political risk		7.16	49.8	0.915
1. Terrorism	0.97			
2. Civil Wars	0.95			
3. Cross cultural riots	0.94			
4. Political Revolution	0.91			
5. Guerrilla warfare	0.88			
6. Factional conflicts	0.72			
7. Nationwide strikes/protests	0.69			
8. Ethnic/Religious turmoil	0.64			
9. Border conflicts	0.63			
B. Globalised socio political risk		3.01	19.5	0.892
1. High inflation rates	0.93			
2. Political leadership struggles	0.91			
3. High external debt service ratio	0.88			
4. Profit reparation restrictions	0.87			
5. Strong nationalisation	0.85			
6. Bureaucratic politics	0.81			
Total variance explained			69.3	

Note: Respondents utilised a five-point Likert scale to indicate their degree of agreement or disagreement with respect to selected items as per following: 1 = very insignificant effect; 2 = somewhat insignificant effect; 3 = neutral effect; 4 = somewhat significant effect; 5 = significant effect.

RISK PERCEPTION FOR VARIOUS COUNTRY DESTINATIONS IN SOUTH ASIA

Respondents were asked about their risk perception towards various countries in the South Asian region. The risk perceptions are built as a combination of the tourist's anxiety towards the happenings in the destination country and the previous experience of the tour operators in handling tourists to these countries. The former category of risk perception is built mostly due to coverage of various incidents in the national and international media whereas the latter risk perception is built over the previous exposure of the respondents in handling tourist groups in that particular country. The respondents were asked to rank the countries in order of difficulty and complexity they place in managing a tour and promoting tourism in the country of origin to that country. This combination offers the respondents to build their risk perceptions based over their experience and opinion of the final customer, i.e. tourist. From the table below we can find that India is the most difficult destination as the perception rank is high for this country, followed by Pakistan and then Srilanka.

TABLE 8: COUNTRY SPECIFIC RISK PERCEPTION

Country	Rank	Mean Rank Score
Multiple Countries	1	4.6
1. India	2	4.3
2. Pakistan	3	3.7
3. Srilanka	4	3.67
4. Bangladesh	5	3.4
5. Nepal	6	3.2
6. Maldives	7	2.1
7. Bhutan	8	2

However the respondent's risk perception of South Asia as a tourist destination is very high (mean score 4.6 in a scale of five points as maximum risk and one as minimum risk). Though country like Bhutan scores minimum (mean score 2) on risk perception but it does not find many number of travellers to this country due to its poor infrastructure, minimal tourism promotion and difficulty in travelling in the terrain of this sub Himalayan country. Maldives with a minimum score of 2.1 on risk perception is the most peaceful destination in the South Asian block. Nepal scores 3.2 in the scale as during the study Nepal had experienced the bloody death of the Royal family and upsurge of the Maoists in the north of Nepal.

From content analysis it is evident that Pakistan and Bangladesh have high risk perception due to growing religious fanaticism, frequent military coup and the countries commitment towards a particular religion and declaring themselves as a country with a particular religious orientation. The second most important factor obtained from the content analysis is the hatred that the local public inherently carry towards the foreign tourist with a different religion whose faith allows certain values that are opposed to the religious practice of the host country.

Many of the respondents feel that the majority of the population of these two countries belongs to a particular religion that is seen as of having blind faith in their religious practice and supporting terrorism at the global level. In the case of India the risk perception arises mostly from the frequency and level of violence and communal riots, the complexity involved due to its vastness and geographic spread, cultural diversity and language problem.

The practice of tourism business in these countries and multiple restrictions regarding the tourist's visits are also key variables for increasing perception of risk while promoting tourism in these countries. In the case of Srilanka, ethnic violence is the major reason for the high risk perception in promoting tourism to this country. Promoting whole South Asia as a composite dream destination seems to be a non-viable proposition at the current level as respondents combined the problems of constituent countries together in giving highest rank to risk perception involved in promoting South Asia as a multiple destination point.

Overall, although respondents agree that perceived socio political risk variables comprising regionalised risk have a significant effect on their firms' profits, as indicated by high average scores, the differences in the mean perceived socio political risk among regions are not found to be statistically significant. On the other hand, the difference in the mean globalised socio political risk scores among the countries is statistically significant.

From a country analysis perspective, there does not appear to be a very high variation regarding respondents' perception of risk, although tourism promoters of India perceive regionalised risk factors as being higher compared to promoters to other countries. From the above analysis, one can propose that although respondents are highly aware of risk factors such as civil wars, terrorism, cross-cultural riots and border conflicts within South Asian countries, they perceive some countries like India and Maldives within the South Asian regions to be attractive and stable enough to contribute positively to their business performance.

This finding indicates that although perceptions of regionalised political risk events can generally be adverse, risks of a national tourism promotion, especially to India is low. Since these risk events mostly involve negative perceptions dealing with international financial transactions such as inflation, profit repatriations, restrictions, and negative world public opinion, they are perceived to be less detrimental to business success than regionalised risk factors as found from the content analysis of the respondent's opinion on the above issue.

Respondents who promote tourism to multiple regions perceive globalised risk factors as having a lower negative influence than those who promote to a single country. These differences may be due to the fact those firms doing business in more than one region may have the ability to direct/ recommend different destinations during periods of perceived political risk in one or more regions. Therefore, globalised risk for multiple-region promoters may not affect their overall risk as much as would single-region promoters.

OTHER PERCEIVED BARRIERS AND THREATS

The summary of the content analysis is in the question 'What kinds of barriers or threats do you feel are of concern to tour operators who do business in South Asian destinations?' are presented in Table 9. Customer feedbacks, compliments and complaints have long been a source of feedback on service organisations' market performance. Although they are not likely to be representative of the complete experiences of respondents with South Asian tourism destinations, these findings do highlight the dimensions of products or services about which they really care. The fact that respondents took time to reply to the open ended question in the survey suggests the attributes are salient in their evaluation of South Asian tourist destinations.

Clearly, the issues of service, crime and safety, economics, health, infrastructure and political and cultural problems appear to be the respondents' overwhelming perceived sources of barriers and threats towards tourism promotion in South Asian markets. The following sections discuss some of these issues and, where applicable, suggest possible steps that planners and managers can take to help rectify the situations.

SERVICE – RELATED ISSUES

If tourism in South Asia is to have long-term success, the level of services and facilities must be tourist-class quality. Currently, many countries in the region lack the capital or expertise to develop a tourism industry from scratch. Instead, they rely on multinational companies through direct foreign ownership or joint venture relationships. This helps provide capital needed for construction and the expertise needed for management. However, it is a commonly held view that when these ventures expire, or when the partnerships break up for a variety of reasons, the service levels tend to fall.

One conclusion is that the provision of quality service is a function of the host country's educational system. Many South Asian countries do not have the technical expertise or educational programmes in place to provide international standard service training for workers in their tourism industries.

In recommending a service quality model for South Asia, it is important to emphasise that making the concept work requires an effective communication strategy to be in place. In other words, it is extremely difficult to determine the success or failure of a program, if customers are not communicating with the service provider. The first requirement is that customers must believe that constant feedback will make a difference. Thus, a process for responding to complaints must be in place, with the customer being aware about how to initiate this process. Without basic grounding in tourists' needs and requirements, service levels are prone to be less desirable resulting in decline in tourist traffic over time.

ECONOMIC ISSUES

Economic risk represents deviations from the proposed growth model of the destination countries. A poor gross domestic product growth rate reduces the attractiveness of the country making foreign institutional investors bring less foreign capital for large infrastructure projects. In order to address the economic issues mentioned by respondents of this study, tourism promoters to South Asia must be assured of institutional structures in various South Asian countries that enforce property rights, settle contract disputes in a short period of time and provide a stable environment for long-term sustainability.

HEALTH ISSUES

While health issues are linked to all forms of development, any development sector that fails to consider health is bound to fail in the long term. Hence as South Asian countries plan to promote their tourism sector, attention must be paid to tourism's impact upon the health of their citizens as well as the need for a health infrastructure to support tourism development. The concern usually is how environmental issues affect the tourism industry and vice versa – how the industry might impact negatively on the environment and thus create a hazard for the health of visitors as well as local citizens.

While some countries in South Asia have begun to institute proper solid waste management practices, many still have difficulty establishing and maintaining the infrastructure and systems necessary for solid waste disposal and collection. In addition, some issues that need to be addressed in tourism planning are poorly treated sewerage on the marine and coastal environments in South Asia and the need for public sewerage system. Furthermore, a good supply of clean water is essential for tourism. Apart from the well-documented health reasons, many tourists to South Asia come from developed countries. Another concern of respondents of this study relates to food safety and hygiene. Supervision of food safety involves inspection of food handling in hotels and restaurants and food preparation for airlines, as well as the regular examination of food handled and supervision and regulation of the numerous street vendors present in every South Asian destination.

TABLE 9: OTHER RISK FACTORS PERCEIVED AS BARRIERS TO TOURISM PROMOTION IN SOUTH ASIA

Reason	*No.	***%	Reason	No.	%
Service related (n=105)			Infrastructural issues (n = 43)		
Inadequate service levels	65	61.9	Inadequate tourism Infrastructure	27	67.5
Untrained ground receivers	50	47.6	Deficient communication facilities	15	34.8
Unfriendly hosts	50	47.6	Primitive conditions at some airports	12	30.0
Aggressive vendors	42	40.0	Inadequate/Poor local transportation	10	23.2
Lack of service ethics	40	38.4			
Slow response phones/faxes	40	38.4	Cultural issues (n = 25)		
Unreliable postal service	35	33.3			
Lack of professionalism by local agents	30	28.6	Cultural differences in conducting business	15	60.0
Lack of direct air services	25	23.8	Language barriers	12	48.0
Erratic airline schedules	20	19.0			
Irregularity of flights to region	18	17.1	Political issues (n = 20)		
Poor follow through by bureaucrats	15	14.3	Government corruption	12	60.0
Hassles at customs and immigration	12	10.4	Inconsistent government polices	10	50.0
Corruption at immigration points	8	7.6	High turnover rates in government positions	8	40.0
			Lack of long-term vision	5	25.0
			Rigorous visa entry requirements	3	15.0
Crime/Safety issues (n=80)			Health issues (n=18)		

Contd...

Category	No.	%
Black market currency trading	43	53.0
Unsafe airline practices	40	50.0
Unsafe local air services	32	40.0
Warfare threats	15	18.8
Crime in the streets	9	11.2
Pickpockets	25	31.2
Economic issues (n=50)		
Current instability	30	60.0
Lack of funding for tourist promotion boards	18	36.0
Lack of marketing support	12	24.0
High cost of air fares	10	20.0
High import duties	8	16.0
High priced ground tour operators	6	12.0
Increasing cost of accommodation	6	12.0
Unenforceable verbal contracts	4	8.0
Epidemics	12	66.0
Droughts	9	50.0
Food quality	8	50.0
Overpopulation in tourist area	4	22.0
Water pollution	2	11.0
Image issues (n=15)		
Perceived distance of Africa	9	60.0
Negative publicity in western press and poor public relations	6	40.0
Unfounded rumours about South Asia	4	26.6
Myths about South Asia	3	20.0

* Some respondents gave multiple answers, hence variation between (n) and No. counts.

** Percentage does not equal 100 due to multiple responses in different categories.

INFRASTRUCTURAL ISSUES

Although South Asian nations possess many natural attractions but by themselves they are insufficient to satisfy the tourist since they must be complemented by other tourist facilities and a supporting infrastructure. However, mass tourism in many South Asian countries is a relatively new activity, which has grown to significant levels over the past decade.

If South Asian countries are to compete successfully with other developing tourist markets, it is imperative that the infrastructure and service requirements, as indicated in the results of this study, are supported. The importance of this is further underscored by the reality that, in addition to airports and telephone/ fax facilities, local excursions and tours are made en route to shops, restaurants and souvenir stands. In effect, the total tourist package should meet certain minimum acceptable standards.

IMAGE ISSUES

The purpose of much destination marketing is to alter the existing image held by the target market segment so that it fits more closely with the destination's desired position. While some fears and concerns of tourists and potential visitors to South Asia may be based on facts, others are a result of inadequate or inaccurate information.

Positive images can be developed through astute advertising of the unique and diverse tourism facilities of a given area. It would, therefore, seem that most marketing techniques aimed at targeted tourist-generating markets, and more specifically travel intermediaries, must also address the perceived image issues identified in this study. For example, the idea that many countries in the South Asian region are relatively safe and inexpensive must be emphasised. Thus, the product strategy challenge for South Asian tourism planners as identified in this research should be the redesign of the tourism experience so that it satisfies not only perceived customer desires but also specific development demands at the same time.

The information revealed in this research could have many practical uses for planning and marketing managers of South Asian destinations to western travellers. As previously mentioned, socio political risk arises from the uncertainty of social and political events which affect business rather than from the events themselves. In simple terms, social and political risk should be treated as business risk brought about by political sources or social environment.

For South Asian countries to successfully promote international tourism in the 21st century and beyond, activities such as research, planning, promotion and education, and infrastructural facilities such as airports and roads must be embarked upon. Perhaps these tasks can be best accomplished through the utilisation of effective and dedicated tourist promotion boards and private participation in tourism promotion by entrepreneurs. This will further facilitate the creation of package tours with attractive schedules conducted on a regional basis, and can encompass the tourist attractions of multiple countries in South Asia. Through effective coordination, their role could be vital in the improvement of facilities for training local personnel for skilled jobs and high-level management positions.

The removal of many of the administrative obstacles to travel cited by respondents to this study like rigorous visa requirements, corruption, inconsistent government policies, etc. would make travel more convenient. Further, liberalisation of entrance formalities could help curb perceptions of hassle at customs and immigration and corruption at checkpoints.

CONCLUSION

This exploratory study has identified two types of socio political risk factors in South Asian region, i.e. regionalised and globalised risk. Regionalised risk is perceived to have higher negative effects on profits than globalised risk. The data also reveal that promoters to multiple destination regions perceive a slightly higher globalised risk than those who promote tourism to single regions. In the tourism literature, little published research focuses on international tourism image as a marketing problem. This study sheds some light in this area by empirically demonstrating that the socio political risk factors in South Asia as perceived by western tourism and travel intermediaries firms contribute negatively to the organisation's performance, leading to negative image formation.

The study attempts to offer guidance to both managers of tourism channel firms and South Asian destination marketing planners for selecting appropriate strategies for increased performance in an intensely competitive environment.

REFERENCES

(1)   Ahmed, Z.U. (1991) *"Marketing Your Community: Correcting a Negative Image"*, **Comell Quarterly**, February, pp. 24 – 27.

(2)   Baglini, N.A. (1976) *'Risk Management in International Corporations'*, **Risk Studies Foundation**, New York.

(3)   Brewer, T.L. (1981) *'Political Risk Assessment for Foreign Direct Investment Decisions: Better Methods for Better Results'*, **Columbia Journal of World Business,** Spring, No. 16, pp. 5 –11.

(4)   Bunn, D.W. and Mustafaoglu, M.M. (1978) *'Forecasting Political Risk'*, **Management Science,** November, pp. 1557 – 1567.

(5)   Cosset, J. C. and de la Rianderie, B. (1985) *'Political Risk and Foreign Exchange Rates: An Efficient Markets Approach'*, **Journal of International Business Studies.**

(6)   Fosu, A.K. (1972) *'Political Instability and Economic Growth'*, **Evidence Development and Cultural Change,** Vol. 40, No. 4.

(7)   Friedmann, R. and Kim, J. (1988) *'Political Risk and International Marketing'*, **Columbia Journal of World Business,** Winter, pp. 63 - 74.

(8)   Gartner, W.C. and Bachri, T. (1994) *'Tour Operators' Role in the Tourism Distribution System: An Indonesian Case Study'*, in Uysal, M. (ed.) **'Global Tourist Behavior',** Haworth Press, pp. 161 - 179.

(9)   Gartner, W.C. (1996) **'Tourism Development: Principles, Processes, and Policies,** Van Nostrand Reinhold, New York.

(10)   Goodrich, J.N. (1978) *'The Relationship Between Preferences for and Perceptions of Vacation Destination: Application of a Choice Model'*, **Journal of Travel Research,** Vol. 28, Fall, pp. 7 -11.

(11)   Hawkins, D.E. and Hudman, L.E. (1989) **'Tourism in Contemporary Society - An Introductory Text'**, Prentice-Hall, Englewood Cliffs NJ, pp. 149 - 161.

(12)   Lax, H.L. (1983) *'Political Risk in the International Oil and Gas Industry'*, **International Human Resources Development Corporation,** Boston, MA.

(13)   McClellan, R.W. and Noe, F.O. (1983) *'Sources of Information and Types of Messages Useful to International Tour Operators from Other Countries'*, **Journal of Travel Research,** Vol. 22, pp. 2 -5.

(14)   Richter, L.K. (1992) *'Political Instability and Tourism in the Third World'*, in Harrison, D. (ed.) **'Tourism and the Less Developed Countries',** Belhaven Press, London, pp. 35 - 46.

(15)   Robocak, S.H. (1971) *'Political Risk: Identification and Assessment'*, **Columbia Journal of World Business,** No. 6, July - August, pp. 6 -20.

(16)   Schmidt, D.A. (1986) *'Analysing Political Risk'*, **Business Horizons,** July-August, pp. 43 - 50.

(17)   Simon, J.D. (1982) *'Political Risk Assessment: Past Trends and Future Prospects'*, **Columbia Journal of World Business,** Fall, pp. 62 - 71.

(18)   Weber, R.P. (1990) **'Basic Content Analysis'**, Sage Publications, London, p.9.

(19)   Weston, F. and Sorge, B. (1972) **'International Business and Multinational Enterprises',** R.D. Irwin, Homewood, II, p.342.

(20)   World Tourism Organisation (WTO) (1977) *'Factors Influencing Travel Demand and Leading to the Redistribution of Tourist Movements'*, **WTO- AVDA,** Madrid, p.16.

(21)   Zikmund, W.G. (1986) **'Exploring Market Research'**, Dryden Press, Chicago, 2nd edn.

SECTION

B

CHAPTER
5

INFORMATION TECHNOLOGY AND CHANGING MARKETING OPPORTUNITIES FOR TOURISM INDUSTRY

SIRAJ CHOUGLE*

PRELUDE

'Information creates knowledge' and therein lies the marketing opportunities – in abundance. This age of Information Revolution has been propelled by the advent of Information Technology leading the world in the 21st century into the **"Knowledge Economy"**.

India has a very special role to play in this century and this economy. This is not what I am saying or any modern day guru has predicted. This has been foretold as long back as the 12th

* Senior Lecturer, Deptt. of Commerce, Maharashtra College of Arts, Science and Commerce, Mumbai (Affiliated to Mumbai University).

century. This was predicted by none other than the great ancient mathematician of the Yadav dynasty, yes, **Bharskeracharya** the great, at Divgiri, better known today as Daulatabad. He predicted the downfall and the subsequent rise of Bharat in his sermon to his pupils of the vihara, just below Ellora. To put it in his own words, "This land will be subjugated by others and it will have its own people to blame. Many yugas will pass. Then it will rise from the ashes. **When**? I have seen in a dream that many, centuries from now the world will be run by great computing machines. Our people will be uniquely placed to dominate this era. The machines will heed the command of unique languages who's syntax will closely resemble that laid down by the great Sanskrit grammarian Panini. All the information that lies within them will be stored in a binary system very similar to that used by great musicologist like Pingala to classify the meters. To function usefully they will need something called algorithms, which has their roots in our ancient mathematics. **When will this happen?** A time will come when all those computing machines around the world will get confused by zeroes, incidentally a concept first given to the world by our own Brahmagupta. When the problem of zeroes threatens to disrupt the world, it will run to our people for help. They will solve the problem, and in the process prove their genius in the era of knowledge. The land will prosper. Our people will once again discover the upanishadic dictum: "Prajnanam Brahma, Knowledge is God".

INTRODUCTION

Information Technology has laid the foundation for the transition of business, being one driven by physical capital to that driven by knowledge capital. Today, companies are subject to intense global competition for survival. Technology is creating a platform independent, low-cost communication infrastructure, which permeates all sectors of the economy with affordable medium for conducting business. Its principal advantage is the ability to seamlessly integrate the entire value chain spanning customers, retailers, distributors, manufacturers, vendors and suppliers of both product and services.

In today's environment the key to success is to capture and retain customer. This will need information systems to develop and integrate customer focus with an accurate understanding of customer behaviour. This will enable to customise product and services and offer greater value at lower cost.

The other key competitive advantage is the differentiation in delivery. Distribution channels driven by technology create a completely new paradigm, i.e., the number of access points for offering product and services to the customer. The maxim is products and services should be available whenever and the customer demands.

In an information technology knowledge economy, virtual assets will replace physical assets and the economies of scarcity will gave way to the economies of abundance. Virtual market-place will be created and virtual organisations will exist.

A PEEP INTO THE TOURISM INDUSTRY

Tourism clearly has been the most remarkable economic and social phenomenon of the last century and so will it be for this century. Already it is considered to be the world's largest industry by WTO. According to WTO Secretariat, international tourist arrival reached 664 million in 1999 and receipts from tourism amounted to US $ 455 billion. Tourism receipts are classified as export and expenditure as import. According to WTO Tourism Report, tourism is enlisted as one of the five top export categories for 83% of the countries and the main source of foreign currency income for at least 38% of them. Tourism, by the end of 1998, had employed

262 million people worldwide or 10.5% of the global workforce and by 2007 it will generate upto 383 million job in totals which means one new job every 2.4 seconds.

For India, as per 1998 figures, tourism accounted for:

▶ 5.6 % of GDP – almost 1,000 billion rupees;

▶ 5.8% of employment – 17.4 million jobs;

▶ 6.4% of capital investment – approx. 250 billion rupees;

▶ 10.8% of export – 231 billion rupees;

which by 2010 will grow to:

▶ 6.6% of GDP – 5000 billion rupees;

▶ 6.8% of employment – 24 million jobs;

▶ 7.6% capital investment – 1300 billion rupees;

▶ 12% of exports – 1600 billion rupees.

With this type of background information, technology can play a vital role in the changing marketing opportunities thrown up by the tourism industry. It has already demonstrated its magical effects.

TOURISM AND INFORMATION TECHNOLOGY

According to the Travel Industry Association of America, in 1999, 16.5 million people used the Internet to make travel reservation in America. More mind boggling is the fact that 50 million people used the internet to research their travel plan, then bought ticket off line. But if seen from a marketing point of view, the statistic touches only the tip of the iceberg, for in USA 65% of all new vehicles are brought as a direct result of research done on internet, but just 5% of all travel booking are done on line. The Research Centre of Bornholm, Denmark estimates an on line travel market of $2 billion that is only just 3% of the market and in India the figures are negligible.

Before we can document the use of information technology in the tourism industry, it would be necessary to understand the profile of the customer behaviour which can then help us in justifying the use of IT for the changing marketing opportunities.

The chief characteristic of the new customer is that they act different, think different, buy different and are moving targets because basically they are early adopters and users of new technology. Today's changing customers:

▶ Have new places to look and book customers;

▶ Are less loyal to brands and tend to select the service providers to match their situation or destination needs;

▶ Know what they want, when, where, how they want it and what price they think it is worth;

▶ Display zero tolerance of delay, or information that is inconsistent or inaccurate;

▶ Increasingly regard access to technology, particularly the Internet, as one of the essential criteria for selection of destination, airlines, hotel, etc.

WEDDING OF INFORMATION TECHNOLOGY WITH CHANGING MARKETING OPPORTUNITIES

Mark Kerr, a marketing expert of Information Society Initiative, UK says, "In the conventional marketing, a brand took twenty years to establish, but the internet backed by the information technology takes only two." This is hard fact that one cannot ignore as the truth can be established by the fact that according to market research by BMRB International the age old brands like British Airways and Thomas Cook in UK arguably one of the best recognised travel brands, in a recent survey scored only 6% and 2% respectively on recognition scale in comparison to the three years old travel website Lastminute. Com, which scored 20%.

This is the indicator that the marketing should change from "Crop" to 'com' business models as:

▶ The information technology is bound to eliminate or redefine roles of the travel agents, global distribution system, reservation call centres, hotel reservation offices and even corporate sales offices.

▶ Brand loyalty will be significantly impacted by the functionality of websites Sites that can provide multiple services will hold customer's loyalty.

▶ The use of smart cards filled with information will give detailed information of the tourist to serve him better.

While absorbing this change, the industry should not lose the sense of hospitality and service which is the core of the industry.

Having information about your guest on a computer is one thing, being able to analyse and use it for the benefit of the customer is another. Ritz Carlton is a good example. Its system stores profiles of 5,00,000 guests worldwide. The guest feels on top of the world when he is told, "Sir, for breakfast you would want your favourite chicken sandwich grilled, with no sauce." The information technology at Ritz Carlton is used by the management to serve its guests with the same choice as any Ritz property without having to ask for.

The advantage of using information technology which creates database management and marketing is that it builds customer loyalty, allows the hotels to identify new customers, helps in revenue stream analysis and reduces long run cost through micro marketing.

TRAVEL PLAN ON THE NET

One of the biggest revolutions is the rise of Internet in the power of choice that the customer has at the click of a mouse. He can compare dozens of hotels, restaurants, holiday packages, and airlines, not just on price but on a dozen other factors.

Promotion of tourism through multimedia: world over countries are using the multimedia effectively to promote tourism with use of CD- ROM base packages. The convincing combination of text video and audio for movie like presentation enhances the interest of the viewer. Not only that, he gets to interact with it to get information on his computer. Tourist offices and exhibitions display touch sensitive screen where the customer can get information at the touch of the screen.

On line Reservation

Travel booking is increasingly migrating on line to the Internet. It is there that the key lies to success or failure of the airline industry.

The Computerised Reservation System (CRS) is in use worldwide for giving information about airline schedules, flight availability, and fare and related services. SABRE, APOLLO, AMADEUS, GALILLEO, WORLDSPAN, etc. help the customers to view and make airline, hotel and car rental reservation directly. They also offer customised options for the customer or travel agent. Customers can even download electronic timetable onto their PC or palmtop and then they can check flight schedules without having to go online.

Hotel on the Net

Room cannot be let for the night that has passed. This is a fact that tonight occupancy no longer exists tomorrow, so can't be sold. Yes, the hotel bedroom is a more perishable commodity than the green grocer's content. Hotels are not only putting their bedroom inventory on the net for regular and advanced booking but are also promoting the fact that discounts are available for late booking. Targeting this type of market are the websites like lateroom.com & lastminute.com in UK and Priceline.com in the USA. Priceline.com in the USA has altogether changed the way marketing is done. Priceline lets the customers name their own price for hotel room. Thereafter it takes the offer to its database and sees if anyone accepts it and comes back to the customer with an offer. Priceline has more than four million customers in the USA and has a deal with Travelocity, which has the largest user base in the Internet travel industry with more than 22 million regular users.

Omite.com is marketed in four countries with one million subscribers in the UK and 1.3 million subscribers in France, Germany and Sweden. Charles Mckee, executive vice-president says, 'we are actually creating opportunities for incremental revenue growth. The likelihood is that a room sold through us world's gone unsold otherwise.'

For smaller hotels worldwide, the information technology with its use of the Net is a boon. Small hotels who do not have partners to do booking for them globally can use website like Goa.com to display their room availability, tariff, special or discounted offer. This will give hotels a virtually worldwide reach. Anyone, anywhere in the entire world can check availability of room of their choice, make a booking and pay online.

Restaurants also go for the Net

Information Technology has given new marketing opportunities to restaurants by redefining the way they plan their promotions, attract customers and maximise their sales. Portals like iDine.com and dine.India.com are designed to enable restaurant operators to fill empty tables by delivery restaurant controlled promotions and incentives to customers.

Such websites will let consumers browse restaurant listings based on varying criteria, make online reservation and also get rewarded for dining. The restaurants can segment customers and engage in one-to-one marketing.

Systems like GO2 and Menus.com offer dining content from wireless phone, where the user can search restaurants by location, cuisine type or specific dish. GO2 online has 3,00,000 restaurants and 2,00,000 menus nationwide giving instant diners information on where and what is nearby to eat from their immediate location.

CONCLUSION

Leisure travel, unlike in the past, would be planned in great detail by tourist as the access to information has grown exponentially and people have limited leisure time which they want to utilise to the fullest extent. With information getting easily accessible, customers are looking for better quality at lower price. More middle class people are going on vacations with their families and the trend is going to bounce up. The people in the business will be forced to come in with schemes which allow benefit to the family as a whole. Again, the barriers between leisure and business travel have broken down. Online reservations are going to increase and only those travel agents who can add value by giving the whole product under one roof are going to survive. Anyone from any remote corner of the world will have instant and authentic information about the happenings in other parts of the globe. Due to the same, even a small habitat which can market itself properly, can take on the might of the traditional leader.

Regardless of technological advancement, technology will only work well with high-personalised service in the tourism industry. Technology should be employed to improve service, not to replace it.

Perhaps, one of the two biggest dangers is to view the use of information superhighway as the solution for all business problems. Instead, it should be viewed as an aid in running a business and not as an end. The real danger is not that computer will begin to think like humans, but that humans will begin to act like computer. Successful corporations will remain 'high touch' while becoming 'high tech' and therein lies the secret.

And finally, to end, what more can be said of the marketing opportunities in general and of tourism in specific, with the aid of information technology, your imagination is the limit. Today you can undertake cyber pilgrimage to any temple in India sitting in your living room, your office or a cyber café, just log on to www.templenet.com and offer your prayers and prasad.

REFERENCES

Books

Tourism Development Principles &Practices- Bhatia A.K.

Tourism & Hotel Industry in India- Anand M.M.

Tourism the Next Generation- Praveen Sethi

Indian Tourism –Beyond the Millennium – Bezaruah M.P.

Travel & Tourism – Jyoti Marwah & Ganguly

Foder's & Lonely Planet Guides

Business @ the Speed of Thought – Bill Gates

Magazines, Journals & Newspapers

Journal of Indian Management

The Southern Economist

Express Travel & Tourism

Express Hotelier & Caterer

Intelligent Hotelier

Business World

The Economics Times

Websites

Mumbainnet.com

Traveljini.com

Hellotraveline.com

Templenet.com

Keralatourism.com

Travelanza.com

Indiatimes.com

CHAPTER

6

HERITAGE HOTELS – A NEW CONCEPT IN TOURISM

ADARSH BATRA*

Today, in India, tourism is recognised as an industry generating a number of economic and social benefits. It creates employment opportunities, augments foreign exchange earnings, and promotes national integration and international understanding. But statistics show that India's total share in the world tourism market is just 0.5 per cent. The Indian government had set itself a target of at least 1 per cent and at least 5 million tourist arrivals by 2000 A.D. To meet the demand of incoming tourists, we will have to increase the availability of rooms. Present hotel chains are on the job of renovation and expansion depending upon their budgets and approval from government. Today, we have 54,000 rooms approved by the government; we must have at least 70,000 rooms more, if we are to meet our target of 5 million tourists. It is a well-known fact that Metros are already full to their capacity and there is a

* Lecturer, Tourism & Travel Management, M.L.N. College, Yamuna Nagar, Haryana.

shortage of land. Apart from this, the construction of a new hotel is a very costly venture. Even the cost of constructing a room for a 5-Star hotel runs in lakhs of rupees.

So these are the problems which are being faced by accommodation sector. To tackle this problem of adding more rooms without construction of a new hotel is the concept of Heritage Hotels. For common man, 'Heritage' stands for the elements gained from the past. Actually, before independence, India had many princely states and rulers. These rulers built many forts and palaces. These old forts and palaces were abandoned a long time ago, finding them incompatible with the changed democratic system. But their charm is being realised now.

Department of Tourism, Government of India is doing sincere efforts to make this idea popular. Former rulers of princely states are being persuaded to convert their princely dwellings into Heritage Hotels. The government is ready to give special incentives in the form of capital subsidies. To carry out the task, Department of Tourism has released guidelines for the recognition of Heritage Hotels all over India. The guidelines will help not only in introducing a certain minimum standard of services and comfort but will also help in tourists' understanding of quality of service.

According to Department of Tourism, 'Heritage Hotels' cover running hotels in palaces/castles/forts/havelis/hunting lodges/residences of any size built prior to 1950. The façade, architectural features and general construction should have the distinctive qualities and ambience in keeping with the traditional way of life of the area. Any extension, improvement, renovation, change in the existing structures should be in keeping with the traditional architectural styles and constructional techniques harmonising the new with the old. Heritage Hotels are sub-classified in three categories.

HERITAGE: These hotels need to be built prior to 1950 and should have 5 rooms (10 beds).

HERITAGE CLASSIC: These hotels need to be built prior to 1935 and should have 45 rooms (30 beds).

HERITAGE GRAND: These hotels need to be built prior to 1920 and should have 25 rooms (50 beds).

The government is ready to give credit for sporting facilities such as golf, boating, fishing or other adventure sports such as ballooning, parasailing, wind-surfing, safari excursions, trekking, etc., and indoor games.

The hotels can be managed and run by the owning family and/ or professionals. There are many Heritage properties in India. About 40 properties are waiting to get approval by the Government. Among them Neemrana Fort Palace on Delhi-Jaipur highway, Lake Palace in Udaipur, Umaid Bhawan Palace in Jodhpur, Lalgarh Palace in Bikaner, Rambagh Palace and Nalagarh fort in Himachal Pradesh, Usha Kiran and Jehan Numa in Madhya Pradesh, and Coconut Lagoon in Kerala are very popular.

Viability of Heritage Hotels carries a lot of weight. Firstly, it is a combination of history, medieval architecture and scenic location that city hotels do not have. That does not mean that these hotels are devoid of modern amenities. The guestrooms have attached bathrooms with modern facilities like flush commodes, washbasins, running hot and cold water, etc.

Secondly, these properties are in a state of despair and will continue if attention is not paid at the right time. Such properties, if further neglected, under sun, sand and rain will go beyond a limit to repair. Conversion of such properties into hotels helps in preservation and saves from further degradation. Thirdly, the former price, if still holding the property, can make good living in new social set-up.

Fourthly, Heritage Hotels are environment friendly though there is a need to maintain gardens and grounds. Actually, these hotels work out to be cheaper than regular hotels. Fifthly, the lower level staff are local residents. Importantly, they have high sense of participation and know local customers and dialects. They just need to be trained in terms of efficiency and courteousness. They should at least understand English.

Sixthly, locations of Heritage Hotels are such that not every tourist is a clientele. Only a particular segment of tourist having sense of appreciation to visit such locations come. Such tourist at one time demands all comforts but is looking for peace and tranquility. Foreign tourist is one such important segment who is very curious to be a part of such location and appreciates the solitude that the place offers.

CHAPTER
7

NEW TOURISM PRODUCT DEVELOPMENT: IDEA GENERATION FOR COMMERCIAL VENTURES

C PANDURANGA BHATTA*

The tourism products need to be diversified and enriched as much as possible to stay ahead of others in the field. India is, and has always been, a storehouse of intellectual and cultural wisdom. Our diversity, cultural richness, and multifarious living ways give us the single distinction of being in a position to offer many unique products to the global community. With competitive lifestyles, breakneck speed of change and an ever-growing need to excel, the thirst for a psychological quencher is at best latent if not already a crying need. Moving from the brand image of being a mysterious land of snake charmers, we must provide new products,

*   Indian Institute of Management, Calcutta.

based on our rich culture, to meet the demand generated by the process of globalisation.

People and customs, myths and legends, rites and rituals, festivals, pilgrim centres, kings and queens of India have rich potential of achieving diversification of tourism products, packages and circuits. Proper researches conducted on these will provide new insights to those who are actively involved in tourism industry and other industries related to tourism, which will help them to introduce qualitative and quantitative changes in their package. This will also help in creation of 'special tourism areas' for investment and development, which will reduce the burden on existing circuits.

Tourism products based on cultural heritage are unending. Packages may range from Emperor 'Ashoka', 'Ayurveda', Museums', 'Game of Chess', 'Poetry' to specific 'Sculptures' – the list is unending. Cultural attraction should be interpreted in such a way as to make them living, vibrant and entertaining. This process of interpretation in tourism is essential. It packages the visit to a place, adding to the quality of the experience.

Cultural tourism products are to be developed in order to assimilate and support local needs and aspirations. These new products must promote local cuisine, the use of local materials and handicrafts, and develop a whole range of other participating tourism services viz. local folkloric performances, hand-crafts demonstrations, cultural and recreational activities, heritage walks, etc. It must also encourage the creation and development of tourism enterprises operated and owned by local people.

This paper makes an attempt to throw light on all the issues identified above.

Tourism industry, like any other industry, is striving for competitive advantage in an increasingly complex world. Achieving such advantage is increasingly tied to knowledge, know-how and other intangibles. Organisations that intend to stay ahead in their field must take the necessary steps to identify their assets and use them to best advantage. Tourism departments and travel agencies have to generate new ideas for achieving diversification of tourism products, packages and circuits along with qualitative and quantitative changes in their packages. It is profitable to prepare packages based on the core competence and strengths of individual states instead of going for common products and packages.

The tourism product needs to be diversified and enriched as much as possible to stay ahead of others in the field. Product development, in any destination, must constantly try to add to the attractions and activities on offer. A lesson may be learnt in this regard from Singapore which lacks outstanding natural resources, and has little in the way of heritage attractions and cultural sites. Yet it has made the most of its shopping, restaurant and entertainment facilities, adding attractions, tours and excursions. Singapore has built, out of apparently very little, a successful and growing tourism sector.

India is, and has always been, a storehouse of intellectual and cultural wisdom. Our diversity, cultural richness, and multifarious living ways give us the single distinction of being in a position to offer many unique products to the global community. With competitive lifestyles, breakneck speed of change and an ever-growing need to excel, the thirst for a psychological quencher is at best latent if not already a crying need. Moving from the brand image of being a mysterious land of snake charmers, we must provide new products, based on our rich cultural heritage, to meet the demand generated by the process of globalisation.

The rich cultural heritage of India has always evoked a sense of great awe among people all over the world. Preserving this heritage should be an integral part of modern tourism management. Tourism in its real sense is an exploration into the mysteries of the nature, society and into the roots of human civilisation. Indian cultural heritage is enormously vast and varied in scope. India's achievements are distinctly unique and original as revealed in art and architecture, religion and philosophy, language and literature, music and dance.

People and customs, myths and legends, rites and rituals, festivals, pilgrim centres, kings and queens of India have rich potentials for achieving diversification of tourism products packages and circuits. Proper researches conducted on these will provide new insights to those who are actively involved in tourism industry and other industries related to tourism, which will help them to introduce qualitative and quantitative changes in their packages. This will help in creation of 'special tourism areas' for investment and development, which will reduce the burden on existing circuits.

The cultural attractions can be classified as hard and soft. The hard attractions include categories like historical sites, museums, architecture, monuments, religious buildings and archaeological sites. The soft attractions include music, drama, poetry, literature, painting, sculpture engravings, herbal medicines, folklore, handicrafts or even heritage walks. Both hard and soft attractions have to be imaginatively combined. Tourism packages should combine one cultural medium with another and incorporate a whole range of lectures, presentations, demonstrations, etc.

Tourism products based on cultural heritage are unending. Packages may range from Emperor 'Ashoka', 'Ayurveda', 'Museums', 'Game of Chess', 'Poetry' to specific 'Sculptures' – the list is unending. The products based on cultural heritage accentuate the relevance of national heritage to everyday life. Cultural attractions should be interpreted in such a way as to make them living, vibrant and entertaining. This process of interpretation in tourism is essential. It packages the visit to a place, adding to the quality of the experience. It can add to the way in which tourists are informed and the degree to which their interest is stimulated. As an example we may illustrate here how the great king of India, namely Ashoka is to be interpreted in order to make a successful package on him. Ashoka (299 BC – 234 BC) was an ancient Indian king of significant merit. He was a versatile genius and one of the most remarkable personalities in world history. He was a great emperor and builder, statesman and administrator, social reformer, philosopher and saint. He was a man of extraordinary energy, ability and power of organisation. He had the courage, confidence, vision and will to provide an administration based purely on genuine human values. Ashoka's love for virtue and his devoted practice through personal example made him an incomparable leader. The glorious emergence of the power of benevolence in Ashoka remains an imperishable asset for humanity.

The skills and knowledge of a tourist guide alone are not enough. Interpretation must adopt a multimedia approach and should include video presentations, talks and lectures, regular guided tours, music and poetry recitals, reconstructions of the past, guided trails and walks, books and published information, posters and postcards, and other printed material, special displays and exhibitions, and signboards and explanatory notices. It is an overall approach.

Tourism markets tend to talk about the new traveller who may be described as cultural traveller. The new traveller is described as better educated, more culturally aware and sensitive, and more curious and analytical. Such travellers look for an alternative to the large mass tourism markets.

They do not want large, modern hotels constructed and equipped according to international norms. They want to stay in small locally owned accommodation units, very much a part of the local community and reflecting local values and ways of life.

This provides an opportunity to the tourism industry to feature and protect local culture and to involve the community in such ways that local people benefit fully.

Cultural tourism products are to be developed in order to assimilate and support local needs and aspirations. These new products must promote local cuisine, the use of local materials and hand-crafts, and develop a whole range of other participating tourism services, viz. local folkloric performance, handicrafts demonstrations, cultural and recreational activities, heritage walks, etc. It must also encourage the creation and development of tourism enterprises operated and owned by local people.

Tourism products at the destination comprise of all those attractions, facilities, and services used or visited during a stay. They also comprise everything that happens to visitors, everything they experience. Tourism products consist of both tangible and intangible components. The natural, cultural and historical resources, infrastructure and superstructure are the tangibles. They can be evaluated, measured and subjected to specific standards of provision, the intangible aspects cannot. They come together to form the atmosphere of a place and create a welcome feeling and overall friendliness. The intangible elements can be said to give the tourist product its life, colour and excitement. All of the tangible aspects, however good, cannot guarantee satisfaction. The way tourists are treated and how they feel, influence decisively on their overall reaction to a place.

The image builds up over the years and it is a product of history, of cultural influences, and also of myth and legend. Also, who else goes there and what they say about the destination also influence the image of a destination. Leading personalities may speak well of a place. If well-known transnational companies set up operations in a country, it too exercises considerable influence. If major tour operators feature it as a part of their programmes, this too contributes to a positive image. It is built up over time, as the result of a constant flow of messages and stimuli. It should be kept at the forefront; people have to keep writing and talking about a product. Once people visit a place they will form their own impressions. They will take an image away with them. What they say and the personal recommendations which they make, exercise a major influence on the product.

Before concluding it is apt to quote the Indian medical genius, viz. Charaka who said: na kinchit anushadham which means there is nothing in this world that cannot be used as medicine. We may modify this and say there is nothing in India that cannot be developed into a tourism product. This should be a morale booster for all those involved in tourism industry.

CHAPTER
8

CREATING A NICHE DESTINATION

S K MISHRA

Marketing is the performance of all the business activities that lead to the flow of goods and services from the manufacturer/ producer to the ultimate consumer/user. Consumers or users form the market. Market = People + Purchasing Power + Motivation. Such being the definitions of marketing and market as laid down by the American Marketing Association (AMA), attempts and efforts have to be made to combine all the marketing activities in such a manner that the target market of people with the purchasing power and motivation can be wooed successfully to accept the marketed product. People with purchasing power can be motivated through marketing efforts. On the same token, people with motivation can also get purchasing power through marketing

*   (Former Professor and Head, Business Administration, Sambalpur University), Professor and Head, Business Administration, Institute of Management and Information Technology, Cuttack.

efforts. Marketing is a very powerful tool, the intelligent use of which can create markets and clinch deals successfully. This suggests that tourists as market can be developed through marketing efforts.

Niche as per the dictionary is 'a recess fixed place on a wall as for holding a statue'. As per Philip and Gary Armstrong, Niche marketing focuses on sub-segments or niches with distinctive traits that may seek a special combination of benefits. Creating a niche destination implies the creation of a destination for the tourist in such a way that it becomes a niche for the tourist. Converting a tourist destination into a niche destination is by no means an easy job. The destination has to become a speciality place in the mind of the tourist to become a niche for him. Such a connotation of the destination is not impossible. High quality marketing efforts can make it feasible.

In order to create a niche destination, the following activities of marketing have to be pursued with all earnestness by the tour operators, the tourism department, the hospitality caterers, and others concerned with the task of hosting, entertaining, and attracting the tourist to the specific destination:

i.   Creating awareness about the destination and its uniqueness through advertising and other promotional efforts to attract the first-time visitor;

ii.   Once the tourist becomes a visitor, services from all quarters must be extended in such unique manner that the tourist must treat them as a speciality regard to the destination;

iii. All efforts should be made to make the services of the destination so very special that they should stand out in the mind of the tourist when he compares them vis-à-vis the same offered at other destinations;

iv.   The visitor not only should be rendered all kinds of services during his visit to the destination, he must also be kept in touch after he leaves;

v.   Maintenance of database and following the tourist through it by remembering him on various occasions is peremptory;

vi. Relationship Marketing and Customer Relationship Management (CRM) are to be given top priority in marketing of tourism services.

The main objective of creating niche destination is not to attract more tourists, which is done through some of the above and several other activities. The specific objective here is to attract the same tourist to the same destination over and over again making the destination a niche for him. Obviously the concept of niche applies only to the repeat visitors. Why at all a tourist would choose the same place for his tour destination again and again when there are so many places of interest in the world. It can happen only when the destination offers him a repeat value or radically different and attractive services over the other places that he might have visited earlier or is considering to visit.

Such speciality services can be offered to the tourist only by rendering cordiality, friendliness, security, and a sense of proximity bereft of any feeling of alienation. These services are the most vital ones in retaining the tourists for the destination to visit again and again. However, it is to be remembered all the time that combination of these services can be effectively delivered not only when the tourist is in the destination but also when he is away from there. The effectiveness of it is realised more when the tourist is pursued intelligently with care when he is away. Such efforts create a sense of belongingness in the tourist for the destination.

To create belongingness in a customer, i.e. tourist, there should be practice of relationship marketing, which is quite different in sense and spirit from transaction marketing. Whereas transaction marketing focuses on single sales, with emphasis on product feature orientation, and is pursued in a short time scale; relationship marketing stresses on customer retention, product benefits, and is pursued in a long time scale. The former has little emphasis on customer service and hardly has any commitment for the customer. Unlike it, the latter is strongly emphatic about customer service and believes in high customer commitment. The former looks forward to moderate customer contact whereas the latter is strongly emphatic about customer contact. Last but not least, relationship marketing strongly advocates quality in everything practised by all concerned in the organisation whereas transaction marketing considers it as a responsibility of the production department. On the whole, relationship marketing is building long-term relations with the customer by understanding his needs and creating additional cross-selling opportunities to bind with the customer more closely. Such efforts beget customer loyalty.

The stage has now been set for further discussion on the application of relationship marketing to tourism for making a destination a niche for the tourist. The objective here is to retain tourists by making them loyal to the destination. The destination with all the services of hospitality, fun and frolic in a package is the product for the tourist. All concerned with the promotion of the product must pay emphatic heed to the destination-oriented product benefits for the tourist on a long-range basis. Every tourist must be treated as "Kamisama" or God. Service to the tourist must be at the top of the menu for everybody concerned with tourism and its promotion at the destination level. That apart, commitment to the tourist as a dignified guest of honor must always be there at the back of mind for all concerned. It is not only service but also high quality service that should be the shibboleth of destination marketing. Prospecting the tourist and following him after his visit are both equally important. Remembering him on some very special occasions that matter to him, help in maintaining a congenial relationship with the tourist. This again has to be done on a long-term basis so that the tourist and the destination remain in close contact with each other for good.

Such efforts alone can make a destination a niche destination which the tourist can consider visiting again.

Prospecting tourists and maintaining post visit contacts are possible by creating database of tourists and the prospects. In the age of Internet, website of the destination has to be there with the pages designed very attractively, which again must be loaded with interesting information. Such pages alone can create a desire in the tourist to visit the place or at least try to know more about it. Because it is interactive, the information feedback to the browsing person must also be very interesting. Internet comes in extremely handy when it comes to relationship marketing and its practice. Best possible services can be provided to the tourist by matching the services with his requirements. With prior knowledge of the tourist's specific requirements of service (s) when in the destination, all efforts can be made ahead of time to make him happy and contented when he is in the destination. These kinds of alterations and additions in services can be made customer-specific to attract him again and again to the destination.

The bottom line of relationship marketing is customer satisfaction leading to customer retention, and finally to more profits. To have this kind of an objective, creating a niche destination is peremptory. The loyal tourists of a niche destination work as great publicity campaigners for the first-timers too.

Customer Relationship Management (CRM) is the key to creating a niche destination successfully. To practise it, the following steps are to be adopted with a positive attitude and proper care:

i.   The customers or tourists have to be segmented and classified so that targeted service marketing approach can be applied effectively;

ii.   There should be better understanding of the needs of the tourist so that they can be better responded to;

iii. Tourist loyalty can be increased if targeted service offerings are extended;

iv. Market trends of tourists and tourism must be analysed on a continual basis to identify the opportunities lying ahead;

v. Attempts to get closer to the customer should be made by either tying up with other partners or opening up own offices in the countries for the tourists; and

vi. Increase tourist satisfaction by giving perfect call centre support.

Customer-oriented behaviour is an obligatory precondition for extension of market share. Such behaviour in tourism helps in creating niche destination too. Niche destination not only helps in steady customer flow by way of loyal customers, it also helps in increasing the tourist flow for the same reason, through word-of-mouth publicity. Hence all attempts must be made to convert a tourist destination into a niche destination to make it a place of great attraction and a home away from home. Only when a destination gives the feeling of home, can the tourist find it a pleasure to go back to the same country or state or city or spot in his holiday errands. To create such a niche destination is by no means an easy task. It takes a lot of thoughtful and concerted planning, and consequent practice on the parts of the tour operators, the transporters, the hoteliers, the fun-providers, and the government, both of the state and the country, which form the iron combination for tourism to make the destination really special in the eyes and minds of the tourist providing him joy for ever. The iron combination should be formed in the pattern of the Japanese iron triangle of business, politicians and bureaucrats, which together with the "Keidanren" (Japan Federation of Economic Organisations) spelt the economic success story of Japan in the last half century. The Japanese economic success was due to the iron will of the Keidanren to pursue one objective at a time with all thrust on it till it reached the pinnacle of success.

This certainly is not impossible if there is a mind on the part of the iron combination to do it in togetherness with a systems approach. The customer or the tourist in this case must come first in the mindset of the iron combination. Importance of the customer is foremost to the success of any economic venture, and tourism, as an industry, is no exception. Marketing concept is as much applicable here as it is in any other industry. It emphasises on the building of brand equity leading to high customer loyalty. In service marketing, retaining the same customers for a considerably long period is a very difficult task, but at the same time the cost of retaining the existing customers is lot less than that for creating new customers. Efforts are to be made by the iron combination in this direction to make the destination a niche for the tourist to visit it over and over again. This can be achieved if the iron combination endeavours to practise relationship marketing and customer relations management in all earnestness by creating proper databases. Now it is up to the iron combination to ponder over it seriously and decide for itself how effective steps can be taken in this direction ultimately to benefit all of them as it is a win-win situation for them all.

CHAPTER
9

TOURISM MARKETING IN INDIA

Tourism has grown from the pursuits of a privileged few to a mass movement of people with the "urge to discover the unknown, to explore new and strange places, to seek changes in environment and to undergo new experiences" (Robinson, 1976, xxi). During the post war period, tourism grew into a mass tourist industry. At the international level, the United Nations has noted the economic and social significance of this growth industry. The first Declaration of the United Nations Manila Conference on World Tourism read:

> *Tourism is considered an activity essential to the life of nations because of its direct effects on the social, cultural, educational and economic sectors of national societies and their international relations.*
>
> **(UN 1981, 5)**

* Professor of Tourism, Madras University, Madras.

Tourism is now an integral part of modern societies. The growth of tourism has converted many communities into destination areas, either as major resorts or as temporary stop-overs for travellers. To make a destination area more appealing and diversified in the competitive tourism market, the industry often creates support facilities and artificial attractions. The objective is to create a more enjoyable and comfortable visit and thereby earn more service by inducing visitors to stay longer. An old maxim in tourism is "the longer they stay the more they spend," thus the industry continues to pursue the objective of enticing visitors to stay.

Tourism comprises

> *the activities of persons travelling to and staying in places outside their usual environment for not more than one consecutive year for leisure, business and other purposes.*

The true basic forms of tourism can be distinguished as: *Domestic tourism* – involving resident of a given country travelling only within his country; *Inbound tourism* – involving non-resident travelling in a given country; and *Outbound tourism* – involving resident travelling in another country. All the three basic forms of tourism can be combined in various ways to derive the following categories of tourism:

a. Internal tourism which comprises of domestic tourism and inbound tourism.

b. National tourism which comprises of domestic tourism and outbound tourism.

c. International tourism which consists of inbound tourism and outbound tourism.

Today tourism has emerged as the fastest growing industry in the world. In the present context, it can no longer be viewed as peripheral or a luxury-oriented activity. The rapid growth of tourism industry makes its study important because of its impact, changing trends and directions. Tourism, despite its phenomenal growth, remains a first world phenomena. One of the declarations of the United Nations World Tourism Conference, held in Manila in October 1980, affirmed that

> *Modern tourism was born but of the application of social policies which led to industrial workers obtaining annual paid holidays and at the same time found its expression through the recognition of the basic human right to rest and leisure.*

Tourism first of all, is a service. So production and consumption take place at the same time. The problems of marketing in tourism are somewhat different from the problems of traditional product marketing.

> *Marketing is a management philosophy which, in light of tourist demand, makes it possible through research, forecasting and selection to place tourism products on the market most in line with the organisation's purpose for the greatest benefit.*
>
> **(Ratandeep Singh, 2000)**

To be successful, an industry must sell its product in the market place. Since tourism as a product is immobile and its potential customers need to build and compare destination images before they travel, some form of intermediary is required. This is the function of the travel agent, who must successfully match a tourist image and tourist product. The industry is also highly dependent on the goodwill and cooperation of host communities. Hence it is the citizen who needs to see how his community is packaged and sold as a tourist product on the world market.

As applied to the tourism industry, the most important function in marketing is to bring about an awareness of the product in the minds of the consumers in the overall market areas. In the present day world, the competition is found to be at peak. This makes it essential that promotional strategies are innovated. It is due to the creative promotional devices that the users always feel satisfied and evince interest in travelling to the same place again and again. The marketing experts also feel that the best and safest way to getting a positive response in the market is to adjust the services offered with the services to be desired. Currently, the magnitude of expectations has been found at peak. We consider marketing as a business tool to manage change. If we succeed in incorporating the important changes in our product mix, the satisfaction index would show positive results vis-a-vis the tourists' influx would move upward.

Of late, marketing operates in a highly competitive environment. The Marketing Information System is supposed to be an important tool used by management to assist in planning for the future, in addition to making an assault on existing and potential problems. The Marketing Research is a major component of MIS. It is simply not information gathering but a valuable contribution to an organisation's understanding of its products, its markets and its overall business strategy. A market oriented or tourist centered plan is the need of hour which requires a well developed research system making available to the tourist organisations a realistic information regarding the users and marketing mix.

Few travel destinations are universally acceptable and popular. Therefore the marketeer can concentrate on selected target groups to whom the product may appeal. Identification of these segments can be alone through market research. Next, to communicate to those segments of populations, the promotional mix is required to include advertising, public relations, sales promotionals, merchandising, etc. The product is then put into the market through different distribution channels. It is also the responsibility of the management to make sure whether the sales graph moves up fast. If there are any difficulties, the marketing plan has to be re-examined and modified according to the feedback from the market. Periodically, some new additions to products must be encouraged, but of course, against the background of emerging new trends in competition, competitors' products, market demand and the mobility of customers. The options are open to replace obsolete ones or to open up new markets. This makes it clear that a clear-cut understanding of market conditions is essential for managing the product in an effective way. The buyer behaviour depends on how well the life-style of customer alters as his income changes and he prefers to travel. Here it is essential that the marketing executives are well aware of the new product opportunities offered by technological advances, innovations in transport, transformation in society and upgradation of ethical values. Noted marketing experts Banker and Anshen opine,

> *the end of the marketing activities is the satisfaction*
> *of human wants*

This makes it clear that the main objective of tourism marketing is the satisfaction of tourists. If we succeed in satisfying the tourists, the expansion of market becomes natural.

India is a tourist destination from ancient times. It is one of the few countries in the world blessed with a tremendous variety of tourist resources. It is the country which always attracted foreign visitors throughout history. Fa-Hien and Hiuen-Tsang from China, Mark Twain and Christian apostles from the West came to India. The Tradition of Travel among the people has continued since then. There are references to pleasure travel as well which was undertaken particularly in the middle ages. But tourism in its modern sense commenced only in the middle of the twentieth century.

The role of tourism was first perceived in India in the year 1945 when a committee under the Chairmanship of Sir John Sergeant, Secretary Department of Education, was appointed to advise the government on the development of tourism. It expressed the unanimous view that it would be in the interest of India to encourage and develop both external and internal tourism. It was the one which suggested the opening of Publicity Bureau in London, New York, and other capitals of the world. As a result, a small tourist traffic branch started functioning under the Ministry of Shipping and Transport in 1949. Later, four tourist offices were set up in Delhi, Calcutta, Bombay and Madras. India was one of the first countries among the newly independent Asian nations to undertake the promotion of international tourism in a professional way. It was the first Asian country to open overseas tourist offices in USA and the United Kingdom as early as 1952 (Pran Nath Seth, 1997). In India, the development of tourist facilities was taken up in a planned manner from 1956 which was the beginning of the second five year plan.

India recognised the economic significance of tourism soon after independence and a separate Department of Tourism was established in the year 1957. The first Tourism Development Council was formed in 1958 as an apex body to associate the State Governments, national carriers, hotels and the travel industry in general with the development of tourism in India. Among the developing countries, India was one of the first to start a Department of Tourism as early as 1958 and set up a marketing section for collection of tourist statistics. Since then, India's Department of Tourism has been publishing its statistical reports annually. England and the European countries started doing it much earlier while developing countries in Asia followed India's lead in this respect (Pran Seth, 1997).

In the early fifties, tourist offices were set up in San Fransisco, Sydney, London, Paris, Colombo, Frankfurt and New York. Although these offices were useful in projecting the new image of independent India, some of the offices were perhaps opened a tourist office in Japan in 1964 when Japan first liberalised its foreign exchange restrictions. These tourists offices were useful in paving the way for tourism from these markets in later decades.

Cultural tourism relating to monuments and an ancient civilisation was the initial thrust of promotion as people in the Western World could more readily identify India with such an image. Hence the image of India was projected as a land of Himalayas, the Ajanta-Ellora, the Taj-Mahal, the Mahabalipuram, etc. But the market planning in the fifties and the sixties was not really feasible because the base of Indian tourism was narrow. The resources for promotion were even more limited and tourism being a new industry, personnel were not well-trained. The broad approach to the development of tourism in the Fourth Plan was, therefore, to expand and improve tourist facilities in order to provide for the needs of the new class of tourists and promote destination traffic.

The beginning of the decade of 1970s opened new avenues for the development of marketing concept in the tourism industry. But by that time, the magnitude of competition was at peak. Moreover, the tourist organisations could not project image of India as a holiday country. The Pacific Visitors Survey conducted by PATA in 1967 revealed that it was only due to image problem that Indian tourism industry had not been successful in raising its contribution to the world tourism. It was a time when Indian Airlines had not bought its Boeings and Airbuses, and the capacity on most routes was limited. That time tourism and civil aviation under Karan Singh became operational. India Tourism Development Corporation was established in 1966 as an autonomous public sector corporation, entrusted with the task of development of infrastructure and promote India as a tourist destination (India at 50, 1997). Meanwhile in the late sixties, the first Director General of Tourism in India along with UN experts on tourism started to promote tourism industry. This resulted in the creation of the Gulmarg Ski Resort and the Kovalam Beach Resort. This period also witnessed the development of Goa as a beach resort and Golden Triangle of Delhi-Agra-Jaipur circuit.

Tourism, civil aviation and the various corporations relating to these activities came under the charge of this ministry. The result was for the first time an integrated marketing plan was developed. Air India joined hands with the Department of Tourism in active promotion of India as a tourist destination. In 1968 a new scheme called **Operation Europe** was launched in Europe to market Indian tourism. Air India made financial contributions to the promotional budget of the Tourist offices and it also allotted targets to their field officers in Europe to sell Indian tourism. More tourist offices were opened in Europe as a result of this scheme. The Tourist officers became **market-oriented** and they started travelling extensively to meet tour operators selling India in major markets. The scheme was considered successful and was later extended to all parts of the world. Indian Airlines also joined by allocating a modest budget for overseas promotion through travel trade press.

Price became an important element in the advertising test to draw customers to India. An attempt was made to project India as a destination by it self and an affordable destination. Advertisements informed people about many attractions other than the Taj in the great subcontinent of India. Special excursion and group fares had been introduced from USA and Europe which made Indian tourist packages attractive and competitive. In Europe, India started marketing inexpensive tours at almost the price of charter tours. In USA, tourist offices kept a list of tours marketed by various tour operators abroad with departure dates. These lists were mailed to people who wrote to tourist offices for information. The idea was to support the marketing efforts of tour operators and to enable the potential tourist to make a quick decision in the choice of his holiday. A favourable climate for India was developing as far as tourism was concerned. The Government of India tourist office in Tokyo opened a tourist information booth in the Indian pavilion at EXPO'70 and distributed millions of pieces of tourism literature in Japanese and other languages.

A market survey was conducted by India in the years 1961-62, 1964-65 and 1972-73 on the behavioural pattern of foreign tourist traffic. The survey revealed that destination traffic to India had risen from 43.2 per cent in 1961 to 73.6 per cent in 1972-73. It indicated that more people would come to India for a destination holiday if right conditions were created. Tourism as an important industry gained recognition since the Fourth Five Year Plan (1969-74). During this period, emphasis was laid on the development of basic infrastructure and categorisation of **destination traffic** as distinct from **transit traffic.** An attempt was also made to develop selected areas of tourism and encourage **charter traffic** (Sharma, 1991:120).

So the market planners in India began to re-orient their thinking on promotion towards developing the Indian tourism product with a new focus on beach and mountain resorts, supported by cultural tourism which is in abundance all over India. Air India also helped by establishing promotional air fairs through IATA from several tourist generating markets taking multi-stopover requirements into account.

During the Fifth Five Year Plan, ITDC was allocated larger funds for developing infrastructure to attract tourists from increasingly affluent countries. At the same time, transportation charges were reduced and facilities developed leading to an increase in tourist arrivals. Tourism continued to attract considerable attention during the Sixth Five Year Plan period due to increasing tourist traffic and foreign exchange earnings. However, it was only during the Seventh Five Year Plan that tourism was assigned the status of an export industry.

The most unique feature of tourism development in India, during the second phase after independence is the use of modern concept of marketing by the tourism planners of the country, both in the Government and private sector. Once again to quote Philip Kotler,

> *The marketing concept holds that the key to achieve organisational goals consists in determining the needs and wants of target markets and delivering the desired satisfactions more effectively and efficiently than competitors.*

The setting up of Maruti-Suzuki Company led to the coming of Japanese to India. This marked the beginning of the opening of the Buddhist Travel Circuits in India. The holding of festivals of India at USSR, UK, USA and Germany during the tenure of Indira Gandhi, created further interest among the international tourists in India as a tourist destination. New Delhi as the venue of 1982 Asiad also served as an influencing factor on the South-East Asian Countries' people to visit India. In the year 1988, the then Prime Minister Rajiv Gandhi set up the National Committee on Tourism to promote international tourism as well as domestic tourism in India (Know India, 1989).

The overseas Tourism Marketing Conference held in Delhi in 1989 was yet another important landmark in India's tourism promotional effort. Besides the travel trade, State Governments were represented in a big way this year. Media representatives were special invitees, besides invitees from other government organisations like Air India, Department of Civil Aviation, Indian Airlines, ITDC, IITTM and others. Our Indian tourist offices in Australia, Japan, Singapore, Thailand, Middle East, Europe and USA outlined the various steps taken to promote the India Tourism product. In keeping with these discussions, the Department of Tourism has set a 15 per cent growth target for 1989 (Know India, April 1989). Fruitful discussions were held amongst the various advertising agencies gathered together to explore still greater areas of cooperation. Favourable responses were received unanimously from the tourist offices for both publications **Know India** as well as **Discover India.**

The management experts realised that if the contribution to the world tourism is to be increased, the solution is to streamline the marketing strategies. This necessitated launching of a national image building and marketing plan in key markets by pooling resources of the various public and private agencies. In the high Himalayas new get away resorts, helicopter services, new winter sports activities were introduced. In Rajasthan, camel safaris, and in the forested heartland of Central India, wildlife sanctuaries have been introduced. More beach resorts were opened up, from Gujarat in the west, in Maharashtra to Goa, Karnataka, Kerala, Tamilnadu, Andhra Pradesh, Orissa and West Bengal. Island tourism too was developed in the Andamans and Lakshadweep in harmony with the fragile and valuable ecology of the area.

In some areas, international assistance is being solicited for a planned development of infrastructure, as on India's Buddhist sector where an Indo-Japanese collaboration of US $ 200 will harmonise the circuit with transport, accommodation, wayside facilities, and landscaping commensurate with atmosphere of the place (Know India). Southern India too began to attract international attraction with the launch of a direct air connection between Madras and London and some other European connections from the first city of the South were expected. The new tourist generating markets particularly in the Middle East, South-East and East Asian countries having a broad spectrum of cultural affinity with India were explored. Ethnic Tourism by launching programme of Discover Your Roots and vigorous marketing of conference and convention traffic were encouraged. Aggressive marketing was required to be taken up in the existing tourist generating markets abroad as well as to explore new markets. It was necessary to reorient the marketing projects and rationalise the locations of the tourist offices abroad keeping in view the market conditions and potential. In order to cater to the need of the professionally trained manpower for tourist marketing, Indian Institute of Tourism and Travel Management was developed as a model institute.

The beginning of the decade of 1990s opened new areas for the development of tourism industry and the marketers were expected to play a vital role. It was felt in this context that aggressive marketing should be preferred to raise the tourist arrivals. In addition to planning the development of tourism products, the promotional strategies were also required to be innovated. This required new developments in the areas like advertisement, publicity, public relations and sales promotion. To popularise India, the Ministry of Tourism launched special promotional programmes with international airlines to help publicise the country and familiarise opinion makers with the product. The department of tourism has also launched a scheme to provide "Assistance for Development of International Tourism (ADIT)" under which it is proposed to meet a part of the expenditure on promotional activities such as research studies, publicity, PR programmes, etc. undertaken, by IATA approved airlines, travel agents/ tour operators and other Department approved segments of the travel trade (Know India). With six months to go before the Department of Tourism's major promotion visit 'India Tourism year 1991' takes off, the officials have swung into action with promotions being launched in India and overseas (Know India – July 1990). The intention of the well thought programme was to create an awareness of the country's tourism product and the newer options being offered by the country. A National Action Plan for Tourism was drawn up in May 1992 and it included a set of strategies for achieving a phenomenal growth in tourist arrivals, foreign exchange earnings and employment generation through tourism. It also aimed to increase India's share of the international tourism market from .40 to 1 per cent by 2000

AD (Annual Report 1999 - 2000, Ministry of Tourism). During this period tourism in India has been recognised as an industry and a new emphasis has been laid on tourism education and training of tourism personnel to serve the new breed of international as well as domestic tourists more effectively and efficiently. Another notable feature of tourism development during the post independence era in India has been the identification and development of new tourist segments and diverse product lines with product items, such as adventure sports as the product line and product items like river rafting, mountaineering, heli-skiing, etc., along with fairs and festivals, heritage and ecotourism, business and convention tourism.

The thrust areas of Eighth Five Year Plan were mainly exploring new source markets in regions and countries having cultural affinity; launching national image building and marketing plans in key markets (India, 1995: 624).

The basic strategy of Ninth Plan was to establish effective coordination with all the relevant agencies so as to achieve synergy in the development of tourism. The approach during the Ninth Plan would be to concentrate on a few selected centres and circuits to achieve balanced development of infrastructure in an integrated manner. As a result, the Central Government assistance to State/U.T. Governments for infrastructure development would be confined to such identified centres and circuits each year till they would be saturated.

The Ninth Plan also gave thrust to exploring new source markets in regions and countries having cultural affinity, launching of national image building and marketing plans in key markets, monitoring and evaluation, creating awareness and public participation (India - 1999).

For the 9th Plan period (1997-2000), the Planning Commission has approved a plan outlay of Rs 793.75 crores for the Ministry of Tourism comprising direct budgetary support of

Rs 485.75 crores and internal and external resources of Rs 308.00 crores to be generated by ITDC (Annual Report 1999-2000, Ministry of Tourism).

The break up of approved outlay is given below:

Sl. No.	Name of the Scheme	Rs in Crores
1.	Infrastructure Development	105.00
2.	Product Development	20.00
3.	Mega Tourism	5.00
4.	Paryatan Bhavan	30.00
5.	Marketing & Publicity	244.43
6.	Manpower Development	60.00
7.	Incentive	15.00
8.	Research, Computerisation & Monitoring	3.00
9.	Organisation	2.00
10.	External Aid through Budget	1.32
	Total	485.75

The above table reveals that the Ministry of Tourism has allotted more money for marketing and publicity.

Annual plan allocation provided by planning commission for the first three years of the 9th Plan is given below.

PLAN OUTLAY

Year	Ministry of Tourism	ITDC	Rs in Crores Total
1997-98	110.35*	70	180.35
1998-99	160.50**	70	230.50
1999-2000	160.50	70	230.50

* Plan Outlay was reduced to Rs100 crores at the time of Revised Estimates.

** Plan Outlay was reduced to Rs 110 crores at the time of Revised Estimates.

PLAN ALLOCATION 1999-2000

Revenue (Promotion and Publicity)	(Rs in Crores)
Domestic Campaign	4.50
Promotion & Publicity	4.00
Hospitality	1.50
Overseas Campaign	67.80
Total	77.80

(*Source:* Annual Report, 1999-2000, Ministry of Tourism)

India is a multi-destination country with a variety of tourist attractions and facilities. It, however, suffers from the problems of economic underdevelopment including inadequate basic infrastructure, lack of hygiene and cleanliness in public places, etc. (Annual Report, Ministry of Tourism 1999-2000, p.31). On the other hand, there is fierce competition in tourist generating markets from several nations for attracting a large share of the traffic to their countries. It is, therefore, necessary for India to strengthen its promotional and marketing efforts continuously even to maintain its existing market share. Steps are, therefore, being taken to develop and implement strategic marketing programmes based on market research and market segmentation analysis. Efforts are also being made to tap new segments and niche markets like Korea, South Africa, Israel, CIS countries, etc.

On 25th January, in the year 1956, tourism was officially recognised as a separate subject by the Government. Therefore it was decided that starting from the Golden Jubilee year of India's Independence, this say should be celebrated as "India Tourism Day". The first ever India Tourism Day was thus celebrated on 25th January 1998. It was also decided that this would be an annual event. Thus the India Tourism Week was celebrated in New Delhi from 19-1-1999 to 25-1-1999. As part of the Tourism Week, the Second India Tourism Expo was organised at Pragati Maidan, New Delhi from 22-1-1999 to 24-1-1999. Various seminars were also organised as part of the India Tourism Week.

To celebrate "Visit India Year" 1999, the Ministry of Tourism presented a spectacular tableau on "Cultural Heritage of India" at the Republic Day Parade 1999 (Annual Report, Ministry of Tourism 1998-1999, p.34). Efforts were being made to focus on cultural heritage as well as pilgrim tourism, extensive use of technology measures to improve tourist information, laying stress on NRI/ethnic segment, special promotional campaigns promoting India in summer and monsoon months, aggressive promotion of yoga and Ayurveda for mental, physical, spiritual health.

Ministry of Tourism's tableau displayed in the Republic Day Parade-2000

Publicity and marketing of Indian tourism is being achieved through the 18 field offices of Ministry of Tourism located in major tourist generating countries. Their efforts are being coordinated and supplemented by the marketing division at the headquarters. Air India and its sales offices abroad also supplement efforts of the Ministry of Tourism by making financial contributions and organising joint promotional events. The publicity efforts of the overseas field offices are also supplemented and integrated with the efforts of Indian missions and other agencies abroad, travel trade and media agencies.

At the initiation of Ministry of Tourism, the participation of travel industry has been made more effective by way of forming 'Experience India Society' to share in fund raising for tourism promotion and marketing as well as extending its expertise to complement and supplement the promotional efforts of the Ministry of Tourism. The Ministry has also taken conscious decision to encourage travel industry to participate in important travel marts and exhibitions held overseas. The travel marts in which the Ministry participated with various other agencies and members of travel trade were WTM, London ITB - Berlin, EIBTM GENEVA. The participation in such fairs gives an opportunity to the overseas trade and consumer promotion and to get a first-hand idea of the pulse of the market. Ministry of Tourism organised the Third Tourism Expo in Pragati Maidan in January 2000 which worked as a platform for exchange of ideas on tourism and showcasing of tourism products to Indian and overseas consumers and trade.

Multifarious fairs and festivals occur throughout the year and are an amalgam of India's rich cultural heritage. They have added a new dimension to the Ministry's promotional efforts. Financial assistance is given to various State Governments. To promote specific fairs, financial assistance is extended in the form of publicity support, particularly "for releasing advertisements, printing publicity material relating to the fairs/festivals and also for creating semi/permanent assets.

Craft melas, apart from preserving the rural traditional crafts, are also a major attraction for tourists. Ministry of Tourism has been supporting the Surajkund Crafts Mela in Haryana, the Shilpgram Crafts Mela in Rajasthan and the Taj Mahotsav and Crafts Mela, Agra to promote the crafts of India as well as to promote tourism to these specific areas.

Hospitality programme is an important element of the marketing process. Under this programme, The Ministry of Tourism invites travel writers, journalists, photographers, TV teams, tour-operators, opinion makers, etc. to effectively project India as an attractive multi-dimensional destination offering a vast range of tourist attractions. In this work regular coordination is maintained with overseas tourist offices, tourist offices in India, Air India, Indian Airlines, foreign airlines, central ministries, e.g.. Home Affairs, Civil Aviation, External Affairs, Information and Broadcasting, Human Resource Development Department of Culture, Environment and Forests, Railways, Archaeological Survey of India and other tourism agencies.

Tourist publicity material is one of the major promotional tools to generate interest in a destination. The tourist publicity material produced by this Ministry has to compete with the best available in the tourist generating markets of the world. In today's highly competitive market-place, it is essential that the quality of material produced, whether films or printed material, is of the highest standard. The Ministry strives to maintain these standards through high quality informative brochures, folders, maps, posters which are distributed through its network of tourist offices in India and abroad for use by tourists.

During the year 1998-99, the Ministry has produced 3 films entitled "India', "Mountain Railway Journeys" and "Himalayan Adventure" to promote different aspects of Indian tourism. The films produced by the Ministry are widely distributed through Government of India tourist offices in India and abroad, to the travel trade and interested organisations linked with tourism promotion.

During 1998-99 an advertising campaign with the catchy "Lives change when people travel" was released in major print media. The aim of the campaign was to create awareness about tourism and its many socio-economic benefits in the domestic tourist market. Ties with the Ministry of Tourism logo and the "Explore India in the Millennium Year" logo were also produced for distribution.

A tourism product cannot be used by everyone, many people cannot afford it. The first step for a marketer, therefore, is to know his product well as well as its advantages, disadvantages, attractions and position vis-a-vis the competitive products. He finds out all this information through research on potential users of the product. In India, the questionnaire method has been more frequently used by Indian Tourism authorities to know the visitors' profile, the places they come from, their expenditure pattern, motivations to come to India, their perceptions, etc.

> *Selling focuses on the needs of seller, marketing focuses on the needs of buyer.*

(Theodore Levitte)

Tourism in India has grown substantially over the previous decades. Although India is a major international tourist destination in South Asia, its share in world tourist arrivals is very meagre. The country attracts only 0.4 per cent of the world's international tourism.

PER CENT CHANGE IN GLOBAL TOURIST ARRIVALS BY REGION OF DESTINATION, 1994-1995

Regions	Tourist Arrival			
	('000) 1994	1995	% change 95/94	% change 94/93
Africa	18477	18800	1.7	0.7
America	107176	111944	4.4	3.0
E.A./Pacific	76973	83624	8.6	10.6
Europe	329819	337240	2.3	5.1
Middle East	9875	11041	11.8	10.0
South Asia	3949	4384	11.0	11.0
World	546269	6E+05	3.8	5.4

(*Source:* WTO, 1996)

100

**PER CENT CHANGE IN GLOBAL TOURIST ARRIVALS BY REGION OF
DESTINATION, 1994-1995 TOURIST ARRIVALS**

Regions	Tourist Arrival			
	('000) 1994	1995	% changes 95/94	% changes 94/93
Bangladesh	140	150	7.1	10.2
India	1886	2122	12.5	6.9
Iran	362	365	0.8	19.1
Maldives	280	324	15.7	16.2
Nepal	327	346	5.8	11.2
Pakistan	454	528	16.3	19.8
Sri Lanka	408	451	10.5	4.1
Others	92	98	6.5	61.4
Total S.Asia	**3949**	**4384**	**11**	**11**

(*Source:* WTO, 1996 p.15)

The entire South Asian Region which accounts for over a
third of the world population does not receive even 2 per cent of
the total foreign tourist arrivals. India's share has come down
from 53.2 per cent in 1994 to 48.40 per cent in 1995. WTO has
predicted that the total volume of tourist traffic by year 2000 will
be 6 million. International tourism in the region was inspired by
strong increase in tourism flow to India and a sustained growth of
long haul leisure travel from traditional European markets and
new emerging markets of the Middle East and East Asia to major
destinations in the region.

**TOURIST ARRIVALS IN INDIA BY BLOCKS OF NATIONALITY
DURING JANUARY TO DECEMBER 1993-95
(INCLUDING NATIONALS OF PAKISTAN AND BANGLADESH)**

Nationality	1993	1994	1995	Percentage Change	
				1994-93	1995-94
North America	20607	232938	267188	13	4.7
Central and South America	13450	11805	16672	-12.2	41.2

Contd...

101

Western Europe	624628	664820	754182	6.4	13.4
Eastern Europe	56709	66060	53275	16.5	-19.4
Africa	61975	64134	87238	3.5	36
West Asia	118223	14096	14748	-3.5	0.6
South Asia	465655	480142	540209	3.1	12.5
South-east Asia	98935	113535	129491	11.4	14.1
East Asia	77058	93844	109916	21.8.	17.1
Australia	39020	43865	49941	12.2	13.9
Grand Total	**1764830**	**1886433**	**2123683**	**6.9**	**12.6**

(*Source:* Department of Tourism, Government of India, Annual Report, March 1996.)

According to Department of Tourism, India receive 2,123 million foreign tourists in 1995 with growth rate of 12.5 per cent. The tourists coming to India are only 0.4 per cent of the world arrivals. Major arrivals come from Europe and South Asian countries with more than 10 per cent of growth rate. In case of percentage change, Central and South America and Africa are main leading regions. Except Eastern European countries, rest of the blocks show positive change in tourists arrivals to India.

International tourism to India has a reasonably good growth since independence. The tourist data shows that the number of foreign tourists arriving in India has registered a phenomenal growth over the years rising from 16,829 arrivals in 1951 to 2,471,848 in 1999.

THE GROWTH PATTERN

Year	Arrivals
1951	16,829
1955	33,269
1960	123,095
1965	147,900
1970	280,821
1975	465,275

Contd...

1980	800,150
1985	900,000
1990	1,329,200
1991	1,236,120
1992	1,434,737
1993	1,442,000
1994	1,866,433
1995	2,123.683
1996	2,283,579
1997	2,374,094
1998	2,358,629
1999	2,471,848

(*Source:* Annual Reports, Ministry of Tourism)

The Indo-Pakistan war of 1971 brought the traffic to a virtual halt, but it revived soon after. Since there was a marked decrease in the growth rate during the period 1980-90, the first major effort to promote this industry was launched with the announcement of 1991 as the 'Visit India' year. The enormous tourist resources were commercialised and tourism declared as an industry which offered a product of marketing. The Latur earthquake, Babri Masjid demolition, bomb blasts in Bombay and the plague epidemic in Surat adversely affected tourist arrivals which increased by only one per cent during 1992 to 1994. For the first time tourist arrivals exceeded two million in 1995 due to the gradual elimination of controls on economy by the Government of India Prime Minister Narasimha Rao in 1991. Because of the various measures adopted by the Ministry of Tourism, the tourist arrivals during the year 1999 registered a positive growth of 4.8% as compared to the corresponding period of previous year (Annual Report, Govt. of India, 1999). India plans to double the number of foreign tourists from 2.3 million in 1996/1997 to more than five million by 2000.

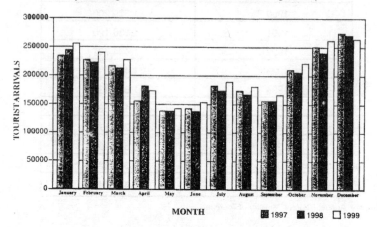

FOREIGN TOURIST ARRIVALS IN INDIA DURING 1997-99
(Including the Nationals of Pakistan and Bangladesh)

MONTH

1997 1998 1999

Countrywise analysis shows the following countries are the top ten markets of India.

INDIA'S TOP TEN MARKETS 1995

S1.No.	Country	Arrivals	Percentage of the Total
1.	United Kingdom	3,00,696	19.2
2.	USA	1,76,482	11.3
3.	Sri Lanka	89,009	5.7
4.	Germany	85,382	5.7
5.	France	73,088	4.7
6.	Japan	63,398	4.1
7.	Canada	56,441	3.6
8.	CIS	56,387	3.6
9.	Singapore	44,187	2.8
10.	Italy	43,500	2.8

(Pran Seth, 1997)

Pattern of traffic has remained more or less the same, occasionally Germany and France exchanging places. Among other primary markets of India are Malaysia, Switzerland, Belgium and Holland. South Africa and Israel are also emerging as important markets.

An analysis of the 1995 international tourist arrivals by the country of residence reveals that visitors from Western Europe accounted for 7,54,182 or 33 per cent, North America 2,67,188 or .7 per cent, West Asia 114,748 or 5 per cent, South Asia 5, 40, 209 or 23 per cent, South-east Asia, 129,449 or 5.6 per cent, Africa 87, 238 or 3.9 per cent, Eastern Europe 53, 275 or 2.3 per cent and Central and South America 16,692 or 0.6 per cent.

The foreign tourist arrivals to the country follow a seasonal pattern. The winter months from October to December constitute the main tourist season in India. The arrivals get reduced to some extent during January to March and reach the lowest level during the summer months of April to June.

THE QUARTERLY INDICES OF SEASONALITY IN FOREIGN TOURIST ARRIVALS

Quarter	Index
January - March	107.8
April - June	77.8
July - September	96.0
October - December	118.4

(Prem Nath Dhar, 2000)

This causes some problems as hotel rooms go abegging during the off-season. Fortunately, due to the recent liberalisation of the Indian economy, a large number of foreign businessmen are visiting India during the off-season.

Over the years foreign exchange earnings from tourism in India have increased significantly and are comparable to some of the merchandise exports of the country. Tourist traffic to India has been increasing at a rapid pace partly due to increased travel round the world and also as a result of the efforts of the Department of Tourism as well as the various wings of travel trade in this country. The foreign exchange earnings from tourist traffic have also proportionally increased. In 1955, the earnings from this source were estimated at Rs 0.6 crores. The earnings during 1956 and

1957 were Rs 5.5 crores and Rs 6 crores respectively. (*Source:* Report on Tourist Traffic Survey 1957, Govt. of India).

Since 1970 the earnings have gone up from Rs 29 crores in 1971-72) to Rs 2,444 crores in 1990-91. Despite this impressive growth, the country's foreign exchange earnings from this sector account for less than one per cent (0.61 per cent in 1990) of the World Tourism Receipts. The rate of growth was much higher in the initial years due to low base, as compared to the growth rate in World Tourism receipts but has since levelled off.

FOREIGN EXCHANGE EARNINGS FROM TOURISM

Year	Tourism Earnings Rs in Crores	% Annual Change
1951-52	7.7	-
1955-56	10.3	7.5
1960-61	16.4	9.7
1965-66	15.6	-1
1970-71	29.0	13.2
1975-76	189.6	45.6
1980-81	11,66.3	43.8
1981-82	1,063.9	-8.8
1982-83	11,30.6	6.3
1983-84	1,225.0	8.3
1984-85	1,300.0	6.1
1985-86	1,460.0	12.3
1986-87	1,780.0	21.9
1987-88	1,890.0	6.2
1988-89	2,103.0	11.3
1989-90	2,456.0	15.0
1990-91	2.444.0	10.0
1995-96	4,000.0	9.0
2000-2001	5,000.0	5.5

(*Source:* Department of Tourism)

The estimated foreign exchange earnings during January to December 1999 were Rs 2,495,55 crores as compared to Rs 2,304,29 crores during the same period of 1998 and registered an increase of 8.3%.

FOREIGN EXCHANGE EARNINGS IN INDIA DURING 1997-1999
(Including the Nationals of Pakistan and Bangladesh)

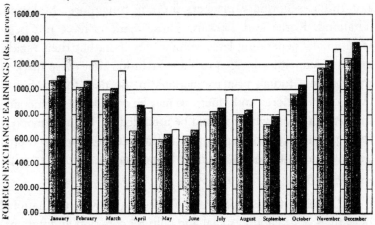

The contribution of international tourism to the Gross National Product (GNP) is one of the standard yardsticks for measuring the economic impact of tourism in the national economy. The ratio of gross foreign exchange earnings from tourism in GNP in India has been increasing rapidly (Prem Nath Dhar 2000).

The average duration of stay of foreign tourists in India is one of the highest in the world. On an average, it exceeds 27 days in the case of non-package tourists and is about 4 days in the case of package tourists. In terms of economic significance, the average per capita expenditure of West Asian tourists exceeds all other visitors (Prem Nath Dhar, 2000).

Travel and Tourism is a mega industry globally and its importance in India is highly significant from the economic standpoint since it makes major contribution to foreign exchange earnings and employment generation. For India, it is the second largest net foreign exchange earner. It is hoped that the initiative taken during the EIMY (Explore India Millennium year) will push up international tourist arrivals. Primary markets for India are USA, UK, Germany, France, Japan, Italy and Canada. Most promotional resources are spent in the primary markets. Secondary markets are those which do not generate very large number of tourists but the numbers are adequate to convince the marketeer that some promotional resources should be allocated to these areas. For India, secondary markets include Singapore, Malaysia, Thailand, Korea and Taiwan. These markets have not been traditionally generating large volumes for India but their rapidly growing economies lead us to the conclusion that these markets may become India's primary markets in the near future. South Africa, Israel, Korea and Mauritius may be considered as emerging markets for India which should be attended to. In these markets their people may be more interested in existing popular tourist destinations but soon they could be persuaded to look at other destinations.

Domestic tourism plays a vital role in achieving the national objectives of promoting social and cultural cohesion and national integration. Its contribution to generation of employment is very high. With the increase in income levels and emergence of a powerful middle class, the potential for domestic tourism has grown substantially during the last few years. India has tremendous potential for domestic tourism. The actual size of the domestic tourism market consists of India's growing urban middle class. Domestic tourism worldwide is often ten to twenty five times larger than international tourism. The volume of domestic tourism may increase in large countries like India and United States of America because of their size and diversity. In India EIMY is also geared to motivate domestic tourist travel within the country (Pran Seth, 1997).

The organisations involved in the development of tourism at the centre are Department of Tourism, Indian Institute of Tourism and Travel Management, National Council for Hotel Management and Catering technology, Indian Tourism

Development Corporation Ltd, Indian Institute Development Corporation Ltd, Indian Institute of Skiing and Mountaineering, National Institute of Water Sports. Some private organisations which have come up like, Federation of Hotels and Restaurants Association, Travel Agents Association of India, Indian Tour Operators' Association and Indian Tourist Transport Operators' Association, provided valuable support to the government machinery.

The Department of Tourism is responsible for the formulation and implementation of policies and programmes for the development of tourism within the country and for attracting foreign tourists to India by way of developing tourism infrastructure, publicity and promotion, dissemination of information, coordination and supervision of activities of various segments of industry such as hotels, travel agencies, tour operators, etc. There are 21 field offices of Department of Tourism in India and 18 in overseas markets to undertake both developmental and promotional activities. While the overseas offices are in constant contact with tourists, travel intermediaries and media to promote tourism in India, the field offices in India provide facilitation services to tourists and coordinate with State Governments for tourism infrastructural development. The overseas tourists offices of the Department of Tourism are the outposts of the Department in the traffic generating markets of the world and their prime function is to develop strategies for market development and implement them to increase the tourist flow to India. The Ministry has also taken a conscious decision to encourage travel industry to participate in important travel marts and exhibitions held overseas. The participation in such fairs gives an opportunity to the overseas trade and consumer promotion and to get a first-hand idea of the pulse of the market.

At the forefront of Indian Tourism is the India Tourism Development Corporation (ITDC) which possesses an elaborate infrastructure of hotels, beach resorts, travel agency, car rental service, convention, conference facilities across the length and breadth of the country with duty free shops offering world class brands to international travellers at all the international airports in India. Formed in 1966, the Corporation has played a strategic and catalytic role in the field of tourism development service. With the advent of ITDC Hotels, for the first time the Indian expertise received emphasis and the foreign tourists were offered an Indian experience, which ranged from authentic Indian entertainment, cultural shows to Indian cuisine (Explore India, Millennium Year, ITDC). ITDC accommodation chain, the Ashok Group, is not only one of the largest but also the most varied. Aiming at the niche markets, Ashok Group of Hotels are classified under the categories: ELITE CLASSIC, and COMFORT'. The corporation has been a market leader in promoting India as a convention destination. In order to consolidate its market share, these facilities are modernised and expanded. The publicity and production division is the only specialised tourism communication agency in the country offering multifarious public relations and advertising services.

The marketing and Hotel Sales Division is responsible for promoting and marketing the services of various ITDC's business groups such as hotels, conferences and conventions, training cell and package holidays. The conference and convention wing of the Division has pioneered convention tourism in India and offers the most comprehensive facilities that match the finest in the world. The Ashok Hotel, New Delhi has one of the largest convention halls in Asia (The Ashok Group, India's host to the world, ITDC). ITDC recognises the fact that all management programmes like total quality management, customer service are essential to a company and can become effective only when backed by a team of total quality people. Manpower Development Centre of ITDC has successfully created a vast reservoir of professionals for the tourism and hospitality industry since its inception. Manpower Development Centre of ITDC has earned a rare distinction of ISO - 9001 for design and implementation of training programmes in hospitality industry. ITDC's Consultancy Services Division provides a complete range of services, including marketing services, supported by expertise in finance, engineering, hoteliering and an in-depth knowledge of the market (Explore India, ITDC).

The concept of Heritage Hotels was introduced with a view to convert the old palaces, havelies, castles, forts and residences built prior to 1950 into accommodation units as these traditional structures reflect the ambience and lifestyle of the bygone era and are immensely popular with the tourists (Tourism Statistical Hand-book - 1997).

> *Travel and tourism with telecommunications and information technology will be one of the main driving force of the twenty-first century global economy.*
> **(Naisbitt, 1994)**

As we are entering the twenty-first century, the world will be increasingly characterised by the penetration of technology in all aspects of our life. In this respect, tourism is inevitably becoming an essential user of the main innovative technologies. While new developments in transportation technology will improve mobility, safety and comfort of tourists travelling by any mode of transport, telecommunications and information technology will radically change the commercial strategies of tourism institutions and business, as well as offer new ways of promoting tourism destinations. With faithfully-designed home pages dedicated to exotic sites becoming the order of the day, marketing tourism is breaking new grounds. Home pages describing various cities and states not only promote India as an important tourist destination but also provide information pertaining to accommodation, travel expenses, and prospective tourist destinations. Another form of marketing tourism is in the form of CD-Roms. Described as "Multimedia encyclopedias on Indian culture, traditions and beliefs," these CD-Roms help visualise symbols of faith in high-quality photographs and illustrations (Website). This is not to say that technology has totally replaced the old methods of marketing and disseminating tourist information. Conventional tools like brochures and pamphlets will continue to be the mainstay of many a small travel agent who cannot afford the adoption of new technology. Further, not all tour operators are well versed with the changing technological trends. Pravin Aggarwal, who provides information on hotel reservation online, says:

> *To avoid dissemination of incomplete and wrong information, it is necessary that technology helps tourism departments not only enhance their level of efficiency, but also add to the steady inflow of tourists.*

Indian Ministry of Tourism has planned to launch a tourism promotion body to promote Indian tourism in the international area. Called 'Destination India', the body will also support and coordinate with individual tourism agencies. Marketing professionals will be roped into the activities of the society which will concentrate on the four main tourism generating markets and also the four biggest users of the Internet: the United States, United Kingdom, Germany and Japan.

> *Markets are volatile. Tourism is a very sensitive phenomenon. Tourism markets are affected by unforeseen natural disaster, political situations, economic changes, the exchange rate, technological changes, fashion, etc. It is essential that we be prepared to cope up with these changes or challenges.*

(Know India, 1996)

The modern marketing principles have helped the developed countries in thriving and getting a respectable position in the world market. In the Indian context, the need of the hour is to adopt market driven approach. This requires to adopt still more innovative promotional measures. The tourist organisations are required to make creativity possible in the marketing decisions. Though India has shown a rapid growth of international tourism, it lags behind many other third world countries in international tourist arrivals (Prem Nath Dhar, 2000). Our country has the ability to offer to the world a haven from political and financial storms that engulf the world from time to time. Hence the future prospects of international tourism in India will depend on the way the tourist product is developed, promoted, marketed and on the political stability and economic atmosphere of the country as a whole.

REFERENCES

REPORTS

Annual Report, 1998-99: Ministry of Tourism, Govt. of India.

Annual Report, 1999-2000: Ministry of Tourism, Govt. of India.

Report on Tourist Traffic Survey 1975: Research and Statistics Unit, Dept. of Tourism, Ministry of Transport and Communications, Government of India at 50, Facts and Figures and Analysis 1947-1997.

India Tourism Development Corporation: The Ashok Group, India's Host to the World.

India Tourism Development Corporation: Experience A Thousand Delights, Explore India, Millennium Year.

India - 1995.

India - 1997.

Tourism Statistical Hand-book 1997, Tamil Nadu, Tourism Department, Government of Tamil Nadu.

Know India: Perspective in Indian Tourism Investment Opportunities.

Know India August 1987: Newsletter on Indian Tourism.

Know India, April 1989: A Report.

Know India: March 1990, July 1990, October 1994, December 1994.

Know India: January 1995, February 1995, March 1995, May 1995, June 1995, July 1995, August 1995, September 1995, November 1995, December 1995.

Know India: February 1996, April 1996, May 1996, June 1996, July 1996, August 1996, September 1996.

BOOKS

Bhatia, A.K. 1983: Tourism Development Principles and Practices, Sterling Publishers (P) Ltd.

Jha, S.M. 1995 : Tourism Marketing, Himalaya Publishing House, Bombay.

Praveen Sethi, 1999: Handbook of Effective Travel and Tourism, Rajat Publication New Delhi.

Praveen Sethi, 1999: Tourism Planning and Development, Rajat Publication, New Delhi.

Praveen Sethi, 2000 : Business Tourism, Rajat Publication, New Delhi.

Pran Nath Seth, 1993 : An Introduction to Travel and Tourism, Sterling Publications (P) Ltd.

Pran Nath Seth, 1997: Successful Tourism Management Volume I, Fundamentals of Tourism, Sterling Publishers (P) Ltd., New Delhi.

Pran Nath Dhar: Successful Tourism Management, Volume II, Tourism Practices Sterling Publishers (P) Ltd., New Delhi.

Pran Nath Dhar, 2000: International Tourism, Emerging Challenges and Future Prospects, Kanishka Publishers, Delhi.

Ratandeep Singh, 1994: Tourism Today, Kanishka Publishers, Delhi.

Ratandeep Singh, 2000: Tourism Marketing: Principles, Policies and Strategies, Kanishka Publishers, Delhi.

Sharma, J.K. 2000: Tourism Planning and Development: A New Perspective, Kanishka Publishers, New Delhi.

CHAPTER
10

USE OF INTERNET FOR PROMOTING ECOTOURISM

M JANKIRAMAN*

World over, consensus is emerging for ecologically sustainable production and consumption. Tourism is part and parcel of this movement. Consumers across the world are changing their buying preferences and consumption habits by switching to products and services that are 'ecologically friendly'. This is a significant and important phenomenon for the providers and marketers of products and services. Although even in the near past, environmental friendliness was used as a differentiating factor, but it is now taking the shape of being a necessary factor. This shift is giving rise to a new product offer called 'Ecotourism'. Though no global initiative presently exists for gathering of ecotourism data, it is considered a speciality segment of the larger 'nature tourism' market. As per the estimates of World Tourism Organisation,

* Associate Professor, Marketing Area, Indian Institute of Management, Prabandh Nagar, Sitapur Road, Lucknow- 226 013.

nature tourism contributes seven per cent of all international travel expenditure (Linderg et al. 1997). From a larger perspective, ecotourism can be looked upon as a mechanism that integrates conservation of natural, cultural, and historical resources and simultaneously providing economic incentive to do so.

Hence, ecotourism can be viewed as a process of creating a hunger for nature, about deterring its negative impact on ecology, culture, and aesthetics (Western 1993). If we recognise this management perspective, marketing of ecotourism becomes an imperative.

This paper explores the opportunities of using Internet for ecotourism promotion and related services. A brief view of the definition of ecotourism is provided for bringing clarity in designing the services offer. Another section presents the opportunities for using, providing and delivery of ecotourism based services. The final section debates certain preconditions and implications regarding the study.

Ecotourism has been defined as, "... travelling to relatively undisturbed or uncontaminated areas with the specific object of studying, admiring and enjoying the scenery, with its plants and animals, as well as any existing cultural manifestations found in these areas (Ceballos- Lasurain, 1983) Boo (1990) defined eco-tourism as "nature tourism that promotes conservation and sustainable development–by generating funds for parks and reserves and communities around them and creating environmental education programmes for tourists and locals." Another definition is, travel which is sensitive to ecological, economic and social conditions of the area being visited and which is managed so as to minimise the negative impact on the environment (Gondwin, 1995). Based on these definitions, it can be observed that, increasingly ecotourism is necessarily becoming a managed tourism. At the macro level there are issues like determination of various impacts which visitors have on the environment and the nature and the actual scale of impact that the ecosystem can sustain. Overall, ecotourism recognises that "natural environment" includes cultural components and that the term 'ecologically sustainable' involves an appropriate return to the local community and long term conservation of the traditions and resources unique to the community.

It is essential to understand that ecotourism is a process and its importance in inducing change in the tourism industry may be more significant than its categorisation as a small niche market. Michael Italk C 1994. Presented are interesting managerial perspectives which indicate that the term 'ecotourism' refers to two different dimensions of tourism. Ecotourism is 'grass or nature' based tourism, which is essentially a form of special interest tourism and refers to a specific market segment and the products are generated for that segment. Ecotourism is any form of tourism development, which is regarded as environmentally friendly. As decision-makers, a manager would be interested in better resources allocation as well as visitors are satisfied.

From the marketing perspective, 'ecotourism' is a distinct product, which may appeal to a set of different consumers. By understanding the consumers, their motivations and characteristics, the managers can create tourist packages, increase net earnings, manage tourism impact and contribute to the conservation of environment. Further, by understanding the consumers, decision-makers can create better tourist packages.

The primary requirement for conservation of ecosystem is communication with the users. Internet can be used as a powerful medium for communicating with ecotourists. Jay and Morad (2001) quoted Wight (1994: 39-55) for principle of sustainable ecotourism:

▶ Involvement of local communities, government, tourists and industry is necessary.

▶ The intrinsic value of the ecosystem should be recognised by all the stakeholders involved.

▶ The natural sustenance level of the ecosystem has to be understood and the carrying capacity has to be given importance.

▶ It is necessary to build conceivers among the stakeholders involved.

▶ Moral and ethical responsibilities towards the ecosystem have to be promoted among the stakeholders.

It is apparent that without communication among the players about the above said principles nothing can be achieved. Hence, Internet can be used as a powerful medium for achieving the principle of ecotourism. As it is a free medium it can facilitate global dialling. The reach can be to almost everyone who has access to a computer and a telephone line. Further, lot of information can be made available in real-time most of the tourists would like to know. With the development of technologies for text chatting, voice chatting and internet telephony, the power of internet as an interactive medium is yet to be encased. In the same context, some television manufacturers have launched a television used for accessing internet. Such changes in the technology could increase the advantage of this medium multi fold. India, with its vast and dense forests to pristine beaches and barren deserts, is an ideal destination for ecotourists. Island destinations like Lakshwadeep, Andaman and Nicobar further add to this diversity. On the cultural front too, India can boast of a wide variety of cultures and traditions, many of which date back to, or are derived from ancient civilisations like Harappa and Mohenjo-Daro. In this context, it is necessary for the tourism industry in India to understand and develop the concept of ecotourism. Marketing will undoubtedly play a significant role in this process.

Another phenomenon that is sweeping across the world and inducing a paradigm shift in the way business is carried out is the information technology revolution. There is almost no industry that has remained unaffected by this revolution. However, the extent to which an entity has benefited from it has largely been a function of how well it has understood the technology and its relevance to business processes. The internet is one aspect of the information technology that has spread rapidly not just among the business firms and industries but also among the households. This makes it an extremely attractive medium for the businesses to conduct their marketing activities. As an information distribution system, the Internet's span and size are immense, its use is not complex or time-consuming, and it is available to all size of firms (Mathur et al., 1998). Business over the Internet is conducted mainly through its graphical portion, the World Wide Web (referred to as the Web). Verity (1996) states that the nature of marketing activities on the Web is attractive, since such Web index saviors as Yahoo! Corp and InfoSeek Corp find that, daily, about 1 million people take 7 million views or "peeks" at Web pages (Mathur et al., 1998). It is extremely convenient for marketers to provide customised and individual-oriented services over the Web at little or no marginal increase in costs. Further, information about individuals can be gleaned from the Internet which makes it an enormously powerful marketing medium (Abela and Sacconaghi, 1997).

It is in this context that through this project we shall study the use of Internet in promoting ecotourism in India. Accordingly, the objectives of this project are as follows:

1. To identify the characteristics of the ecotourist segment and their preferences.

2. To understand the information needs of the ecotourist that the marketers of tourism are expected to provide.

3. To explore the possibilities and suggest ways to exploit the Internet as a medium for conducting marketing activities related to ecotourism.

RESEARCH METHODOLOGY

The project involved both primary as well as secondary research though a major part of this study is based on data gathered from secondary sources.

Considerable amount of research has been conducted in the past regarding issues related to marketing of services and also, to some extent, marketing of tourism. But ecotourism being a relatively recent concept, not many studies have been published on issues specific to marketing of ecotourism. The Internet, however, is a useful source for this and has been used for obtaining data regarding the characteristics of the ecotourism segment.

In the initial stages of the project, the Internet was used to obtain information regarding the concept of ecotourism, profile of ecotourists and get an understanding of their requirements in terms of the desired experience. Published studies on services in general and tourism in particular have also been used to provide information on the tourism market.

Articles related to Internet and Web based marketing published in various journals and other publications have been used extensively to understand the nuances and peculiarities of the medium in the context of marketing activities.

Before integrating the e-marketing possibilities with the requirements of the tourists, it is necessary to know the needs of the ecotourists in terms of information and services that are amenable for delivery over the Internet. These details were obtained through primary research by way of a survey conducted over the Internet.

The data obtained from the above sources were then analysed and adapted for promoting ecotourism using the Internet.

SAMPLE FRAME AND SURVEY

The primary research was conducted with the aim of understanding the information and service needs of the ecotourists. For this reason the survey included only ecotourists who were contacted through e-mail.

Sample Frame: All individuals whose names appeared on the bulletin boards/ chatsites/ discussion forums hosted by travel related websites.

Prospective respondents were identified through public bulletin boards and discussion forums hosted by travel related websites. The websites used in this survey were:

► www.excite.com

► www.yahoo.com

► www.booksotes.com

► www.lonelyplanet.com

► www.ecotourism.org

Among the individuals who were listed on the above sites, only those individuals who were ecotourists and were ready to participate in the survey, were to be considered as respondents.

Totally 103 persons were contacted through e-mail. The criteria for being classified as an ecotourist were outlined in the mail and the decision whether or not to be considered as an ecotourist was then left to the individual. The mail also contained a question regarding the readiness of the individual to participate in subsequent surveys. The survey sample then consisted of those individuals who satisfied both conditions, namely considered themselves to be ecotourists and were ready to participate in the main survey.

34 persons replied indicating readiness to participate in the survey. However, only 32 of them qualified themselves as ecotourists and were hence considered for the final survey.

These respondents were then mailed a questionnaire consisting of 12 questions apart from demographics. The length of the questionnaire was deliberately kept short keeping in mind that the questions were open-ended and a longer questionnaire could induce boredom in the respondents. The questions had to be open-ended since close-ended questions would require HTML coding of the questionnaire.

Of the 32 questionnaires sent, all were retained duly filled up and none of the responses were rejected on account of incomplete or incorrect information.

The questionnaire elicited information mainly regarding frequency of travel, sources of information and the use of Internet.

LITERATURE SURVEY

Tourism, in general, is a leisure service and the promotion of leisure services involves both, economic and emotional aspects of consumer responses. The decision of using price-oriented or non-price sales promotional techniques depends on the target audience. Wakefield and Bush (1998) have stated that household income will have a negative effect on price consciousness, and price consciousness will have negative effect on patronage frequency. In this regard the elderly population is an attractive segment due to relatively higher levels of discretionary income and also because they possess more time at their disposal for leisure oriented activities. Dychtwald (1989) states that even within the elderly population there is great diversity in terms of their attitude and behaviour (Sherman et al., 1998). Unlike the traditional elderly, new-age elderly perceive themselves as younger in age and outlook (irrespective of their chronological age), more in control of their lives, and more self-confident (Sherman et al., 1998). The new-age elderly that Sherman et al., refer to are less receptive to trips where everything is "done for them" – and there is a need for presenting better "experiences" rather than "price packages" for this group (Sherman et al., 1998). Though the elderly population is an important segment of the ecotourism market, the scope of ecotourism is much wider. A study by HLA and ARA consulting firms of N. America regarding the characteristics of an ecotourist reveal interesting observations (The Ecotourism Society, 1998):

1. The age of an ecotourist is generally between 35 to 50 years.

2. Gender-wise, both males and females comprise equal proportions, though there is a clear difference in activities.

3. The education level of an ecotourist is relatively higher. 82% of the ecotourists interviewed were educated till the level of college graduation or higher and showed higher levels of income.

4. 73% of the ecotourists preferred to travel alone or as a couple, with the remaining opting to take their family along or travelling in groups.

5. Around 50% of the ecotourists preferred trips lasting 8 to 14 days or more.

6. In general, these tourists spend more per trip than their conventional counterparts. 26% of the respondents said that they spent in excess of US$ 1500 per trip at the destination, i.e. excluding the airfare.

7. The ecotourists' concerns related more to nature and culture related offerings rather than plush accommodation and luxury transportation.

8. The main motivations behind ecotourism were the enjoyment of scenery, nature and new experiences and places.

9. Ecotourists displayed high levels of environmental awareness and conscience compared to the conventional tourist.

The higher levels of education and income are a pointer to the possibility that the penetration of Internet as a mode of communication will be high among this segment. When people are preparing for trips they would want to know what kind of tours, accommodations, services are available. The Internet provides seemingly direct contact to services that are off the beaten track. Elderly people, perhaps because they have more time available for Web exploration and surfing, represent the fastest growing segment of Internet users (Huff et al., 1998). Hannon (1996) stated that Internet access from home is predicted to increase from almost 11 million people in January 1996 to 50 million people by the year 2000 (Mathur et al., 1998). Pre-sale marketing is part of the nature and role of services marketing (Berry and Parasuraman, 1991). The Internet reduces the risk factor in the consumption of services by adding value to the information search (Mathur et al., 1998). With increasing levels of awareness and demand for information, companies that do not want to participate in Internet commerce may be forced to do so by competitors or customers (Ghosh, 1998).

In spite of the attractiveness of employing the Internet as a marketing medium, few markets have met the challenge of doing so successfully. In a survey of the websites of all the consumer companies in the Fortune 500 conducted by Abela and Sacconaghi, Jr. (1997), it was found that many do not even try to gather information about individuals and those that do, tend to ask only for the kind of data already available through conventional market research. A poor web page/site will, if it is ever found, be quickly surfed over and never revisited (Bickerstaff, 1996).

However, most good websites:

1. are aesthetically pleasing but without excessive use of graphics;

2. function well on a variety of platforms, browser types, screen sizes, etc.;

3. are easy to navigate;

4. are readily accessible;

5. have interesting and useful content;

6. are frequently enhanced and updated;

7. feature a human touch;

8. contain elements of interactivity;

9. observe conventions of Netiquette (etiquette on the Internet).

There are various potential measures of success, including the number of hits, the number of visitors, and the number of online transactions but the appropriate measure of success depends in part on the objective of the site (Bickerstaff, 1996). Ecotourists are concerned about the environment and conservation and as responsible travellers, they want to ensure that their travels are environmentally-friendly. Ecotourism sites should concentrate on addressing ecotourists' primary interests – nature and the environment. Since ecotourists place great emphasis on learning, it is important that the ecotourism operator provide factual information about the region's natural and environmental history, problems and attractions (karwacki, 1998).

As business increasingly uses the Internet for conducting activities, it becomes necessary to understand the medium so that value can be created and delivered over the Internet. Rayport and Sviokla (1995) refer to this new information world as marketspace to distinguish it from the physical world, which they refer to as market-place. Their findings indicate that managers often use information that they capture on inventory, production or logistics to help monitor or control those processes, but they rarely use information itself to create new value for the customer. Creating value in any stage of a virtual value chain (the value chain in the marketspace) involves a sequence of five activities: gathering, organising, selecting, synthesising and distributing information (Rayport and Sviokla, 1995). Companies adopt the value adding information processes in three stages: visibility, in which companies acquire an ability to "see" physical operations; substitute virtual activities for physical ones creating a parallel value chain in the marketspace; and finally building new customer relationships through the marketspace (Rayport and Sviokla, 1995).

ANALYSIS OF PROBLEM/ DATA

Though the sample size was small (32), the e-mail data collected in the survey gave some useful details about the ecotourists. The results have been summarised below:

EXHIBIT 1: RESULTS OF SURVEY

▶ Average number of trips in past 2 years	
▶ Sources referred to for travel related information	
Internet	94%
Books/ Brochures/ Travel Guides	75%
Friends/Word-of-mouth	75%
Travel Agents	53%
Magazines	28%
Others (Newspapers, TV Shows)	16%
▶ Most reliable sources among above sources	
Internet	13%

Contd...

Books/Brochures/Travel Guides	28%
Friends/Word-of-mouth	53%
Others	6%

▶ Ever used Internet as source of Information in the past

▶ Proportion who found Internet reliable

▶ How important is speed of access to websites?

Very	41%
Somewhat	59%

▶ Proportion who are satisfied with current speed

▶ Type of information sought from the Internet

Outdoor activities/Places of natural beauty	75%
Other people's experiences	75%
Historical/ Cultural details	56%
Food/ Accommodation details	37%
Flight schedules/ Air fares	16%
Other details	19%

▶ Proportion who were satisfied with current information available on the Internet — 41%

▶ Type of additional information required

Historical/ Cultural information	41%
Details of wildlife	19%
Other	40%

▶ Proportion who felt advertisements on websites are a nuisance — 81%

▶ Average age of respondents — 40 years

▶ Education level of respondents

Below Graduation	3%
Graduation	78%
Postgraduation	19%

RECOMMENDATIONS

The needs of an ecotourist in terms of information and services and the potential of Internet in providing information at low costs provides an excellent opportunity for employing the Internet as a marketing medium. The marketeer justifies its use through high levels of reach and coverage of the target segment. This marketspace can be used to create a virtual value chain, which elicits information from the ecotourists and uses the same to create more value for them. However, the potential of Internet is not limited to just hosting websites though it is an important aspect. A useful framework for realising the full potential of the Internet for marketing purposes has been provided by Rayport and Sviokla (1995) in the form of exploiting the virtual value chain through visibility, mirroring capability and new customer relationships.

Visibility

This is the process through which companies keep track of the physical activities by collecting information about the progress on different stages in the physical value chain. By having access to the situation across the value chain simultaneously at one place, the manager is in a position to see the entire business process as an integrated entity and take decisions accordingly. Frito-Lay, world leader in the snack-foods industry, makes extensive use of its information system to collect data on sales of products daily, store by store, across the United States and feed it to the company. Information regarding competitors' activities is also captured and by combining this field level data from each stage in the value chain, managers at Frito are in a better position to take decisions related to logistics.

In ecotourism, there is no tangible product on offer as in the case of Frito, whose movement along the value chain needs to be monitored. Instead, what needs to be closely monitored is the movement of the tourist along the value chain of experiences, which together determine the quality of the tourist's overall tourism experience. This throws up another issue: what is the overall tourism experience? We shall define this term as "the set of all experiences that the tourist undergoes from the time he thinks of visiting a destination till the time he goes back from his visit and forgets about the destination". This not only calls for a change in our attitude towards the tourists but also requires the various tourism related industries to go in for a greater degree of integration. This is because in the new setting an individual entity in the tourism industry, say a hotel, will assume responsibility for the satisfaction of the tourist in areas much beyond conventional limits. For example, if the plane by which a tourist has arrived has been delayed by a few hours causing him to get irritated, the hotel in which he is checking-in can make amends by accordingly altering the services provided. This would be possible only if the hotel comes to know before hand about the delay in the flight and makes the necessary arrangements in advance to receive the disgruntled tourist. The Internet, or the marketspace, can play a vital role in such situations by providing critical information on a real-time basis. This also calls for a greater degree of integration and cooperation among the industries involved (the airlines and hotel industry in the above example) since it not only requires the hotel industry to keep track of information on the Internet but also requires the airlines industry to feed the information regularly.

Mirroring Capability

In this process, companies begin to shift value-adding activities from the market-place on to the marketspace. These activities can be performed better, faster, more economically and with more flexibility on the Internet.

In the context of ecotourism, this can be applied to activities ranging from simple ones like providing brochures to more complex ones like virtual tours for planning itineraries, making reservations and making financial transactions over the Internet. Each of these activities can be customised to suit individual requirements of the tourists at little or no additional cost to the service provider, which is not always possible in the market-place. For example, while providing brochure over the Internet, the contents of the brochure can easily be altered to include details that the particular tourist is interested in but is not a part of the standard brochure. Doing this in the physical world means designing and printing a different brochure for each customer. The costs and time involved make this infeasible. On the Internet, however, all one requires to do is to maintain a database of the information and images that would satisfy different tourists. Then depending on the area in which the customer is interested in, the necessary details can be combined and delivered to the receiver. The areas of interest to the tourists can be determined through explicit request that the tourist is required to make. An alternative method is to employ the technology of "cookies" to keep track of the customer's interests. A cookie is an HTML code that can be embedded in a website; when a person is followed during his visit to the website, this information is stored in the coded form in the visitor's hard disk. The next time that this person visits the website, the "cookie" searches and retrieves information that it had stored during the earlier visit. Using this data as an indicator of the preferences of that visitor, the information provided can be suitably altered. In this way, the marginal cost of preparing an additional brochure is negligible and the time involved is limited only by the speed of the microprocessors involved and transmission media. This shows how, even in seemingly marginal activities, large amounts of savings can be generated while at the same time greatly enhancing the value delivered to the tourist.

New Customer Relationships

This involves contacting and acquiring the loyalty of new customers and generating additional business in the process. It requires developing an interface with the prospective customer, understanding his needs and requirements and fulfilling those needs using the Internet.

Ecotourists, as determined in the survey, are primarily interested in information related to sites of natural beauty and the history and culture of the destination they intend to visit. The results of the survey also indicate an opportunity in this area since most of the respondents have indicated that information about the history and culture of different places is lacking. By providing this information, marketers can hope to attract more number of visitors to the websites. Once the prospective tourists are attracted to the website, the job of the marketer turns to developing a value-based relationship with the customer and convincing him to visit the destination. This gives rise to the need of the marketer/ provider of the service to remain accessible to the tourist. This can be done either through a link for communication through e-mail or by hosting a public message board/ chat room. In either case, the host (the provider of the service) has to be responsive to any query or attempt by the customer to contact him.

A study of the Indian tourism websites shows that although some are visually appealing, the information provided in most sites is of very little value and often outdated. Four of these sites were randomly chosen by the author[1], and queries regarding the approximate cost of a non-standard tour were sent through the e-mail link on the websites. As expected, the queries were neither answered nor acknowledged. This attitude creates a strong dissatisfaction among the customers and defeats the very purpose of hosting a website. On the other hand, a similar survey of four websites[2] that were mentioned as favourites among the respondents of the survey, yielded drastically different results. Similar queries

---

1   These were sites of Goa, HP, Rajasthan and Kerala accessed from www.inetindia.com/travel/indes.html

2   These sites were: www.lonelyplanet.com, www.globaltrip.com, www.foders.com, www.frommers.com

sent through these websites were replied with detailed information within 24 hours. In one case where the website contacted did not have the required answer, the reply gave directions as to where the information could be obtained along with an apology for not being able to reply with full details. This kind of alacrity is essential for building a relationship with the customer which can prove to be profitable in the long run. Hosting chat rooms or public message boards is a popular method since it allows various tourists to exchange views and experiences with each other. As determined in the survey, word-of-mouth/ friends was considered the most reliable source of information. Free exchange of views and experiences through such forums accelerates the word-of-mouth process. To control and limit the damages in case of negative views, the host should also actively participate in these discussions. This will provide an opportunity to give accurate information, identify causes of dissatisfaction, areas for improvement, keep the people informed about corrective actions being taken and generate greater involvement of the tourists by creating a community like feeling. This is a profitable proposition since an enduring involvement with a category in leisure services has a positive effect on patronage frequency, and patronage frequency has a negative effect on price consciousness (Wakefield and Bush, 1998).

The use of Internet can also be extended to activities that eliminate the need for intermediaries like travel agents. However, in light of the findings that travel agents are still looked upon as a reliable source of information, efforts should be made to periodically provide them with updated and relevant information which they can use to attract visitors.

Regarding the design of websites, exhibit 2 gives a simple and useful framework.

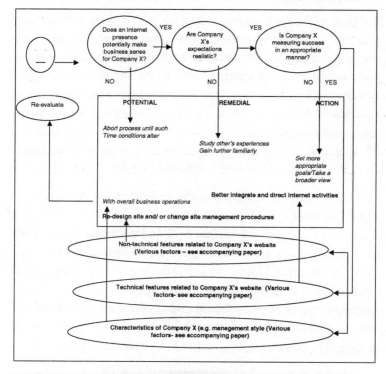

EXHIBIT 2: A SUGGESTED POST-MORTEM PROCEDURE FOR AN APPARENTLY "DUD" COMPANY WEBSITE
COPYRIGHT 1996 MEET THE PEOPLE PVT. LTD

IMPLICATIONS FOR IMPLEMENTATION

The Internet is a powerful tool that can be used for marketing and promoting ecotourism. But in order to make optimum use of the medium it needs to be understood before being deployed. The groundwork has to be done in terms of strategic alignment of the industry to exploit the full potential of the Internet. There should be a great degree of integration and/or cooperation among the entire chain of industries that contribute to the tourists' overall experience. These include tourism development corporations, travel agencies, tour operators, airlines, hotels, resorts, taxi unions and wildlife/ forest authorities. The Internet can play the role of the common thread that runs through all of them and integrates their activities. Each entity in this chain should consider itself responsible for the satisfaction of the tourist across the overall experience. This is because if it makes no effort to keep the tourist totally satisfied and sticks to its conventional limits of responsibility, it is bound to lose the customer even if it provides excellent services but some other entity in the chain delivers a faulty service.

The integration between the industries mentioned above should also include the maintenance of a common database of the tourists and their individual likes and preferences. Currently, such practices exist only among individual firms like hotels (e.g. The Taj Group of Hotels) and airlines (e.g. British Airways). By pooling their resources, more relevant and greater amount of information can be warehoused and used for enhanced levels of service delivery. This can serve as a differentiating factor and a competitive advantage over other tourist destinations.

Before serving the tourist with information and services, it is essential to understand what the tourist's needs are. At present, there is not much initiative to identify the various segments and their characteristics, in the tourism market. All the tourists are treated as similar in terms of the desired experience and no attempt is made to understand the underlying differences in motivations and preferences and position different destinations accordingly. A few examples are notable for their efforts in this direction. The Kerala based Casino group of resorts owned by the Dominic Brothers is one such example. They have successfully positioned their resorts as exclusive, up-market eco-resorts targeted at the environmentally aware, high spending tourist. Being an eco-resort, minimal facilities are offered in terms of luxuries. At the same time, an exclusive positioning allows them to charge a premium and increase their earnings without increasing the number of tourists thus maintaining the sustainability of the environment.

Tourism forecasting through scientific methods is another area that needs attention. This information is to enable the use of proper technology at the proper scale. Moreover, forecasting accuracy is particularly important when forecasting tourism demand on account of the perishable nature of the product (Witt and Witt, 1995). Forecasting techniques like Naïve 1, Naïve 2, Exponential smoothing, Trend Curve Analysis, Compertz, Stepwise Autoregression, and Econometric models are available for the purpose (Martin and Witt, 1989). It has also been found that several of the simple forecasting methods produce more accurate forecasts than econometric forecasts (Martin and Witt, 1989). These models can be used in the specific context of ecotourism to enable a better decision making process. Qualitative forecasting techniques like Delphi and Scenario are available (Witt and Witt, 1995) for forecasting future trends on the ecotourism front depending on the changes in attitudes and preferences of the tourists.

Unlike other conventional media, the Internet is still evolving and it may not be possible to understand it in its entirety. This should not, however, discourage the Indian tourism industry from experimenting and attempting to exploit the medium to its fullest possible extent.

LIMITATIONS AND SCOPE FOR FURTHER WORK/STUDY

This project is based largely on secondary data. The sample size for the survey conducted, though large enough for statistical operations (more than 30), is too small to be a true representative of the ecotourist population. Hence the results derived through this survey are bound to have a high degree of error. The decision to classify tourists as ecotourists or otherwise was also left to the respondents themselves, and there is a possible room for error if the respondent had wrongly qualified himself as an ecotourist and got included in the final survey.

More detailed studies need to be undertaken to identify the ecotourist segment and determine their characteristics for use by marketers and providers of ecotourism.

The ways that have been suggested for using the Internet for marketing purpose are just suggestive and not exhaustive. A lot is dependent on the ingenuity of individual firms in using the Internet as an effective marketing medium.

Using the Internet as a marketing medium is a fairly recent concept and there is no objective method of measuring the effectiveness of the same. Further research is required in the area of Internet behaviour or "browsing" behaviour of people to devise methods for measuring its effectiveness.

REFERENCES

1. Abela A.V. and Saccomagjo A.M., Jr. (1997), "Value Exchange: The Secret of Building Customer Relationships Online". The McKinsey Quarterly, No.2, pp. 216 – 219.

2. Berry L.L., and Parasurraman A. (1991), Marketing Services: Competing through Quality, The Free Press, New York, N, pp. 7.

3. Bickerstaff B. (1996), "Marketing on the Internet and World Wide Web", http:// www.meetoz.com.au/intconf.html.

4. Ceballos- Lascurain H. (1983), "What is Ecotourism?", http://www.up.ac.za/science/eco/ecotour.htm.

5. Ghosh S. (1998), "Making Business Sense of the Internet", Harvard Business Review, March – April, pp. 126- 135.

6. Huff S.L., Koltermann D., and Glista J. (1998), "Settlers, not Surfers", lvey Business Quarterly, Simmer, pp. 45- 49.

7. Karwacki J. (1998), "A Guide for Ecotourism Operators", http:// www.planeta.com/mader/planeta/0597operators.html.

8.   Lindberg K., Furze B., Staff M., and Black R. (1997), "Ecotourism Statistical Fact Sheet". http:// www.ecotourism.org/datafr/html.

9.   Martin C.A. and Witt S.F. (1989), "Forecasting Tourism Demand: A Comparison of the Accuracy of Several Quantitative Methods", International Journal of Forecasting 5, pp.7-19.

10. Mathur L.K., Mathur I., and Gleason K.C. (1998), "Services Advertising and Providing Services on the Internet", The Journal of Services Marketing, Vol. 12, pp. 334-347.

11. Rayport J.F. and Sviokla J. (1995), "Exploiting the Virtual Value Chain", Harvard Business Review, November – December, pp. 75-85.

12. Reingold L. (1993), "Ecotourism Statistical Fact Sheet", http:// www.ecotourism.org/datafr/html.

13. Sherman E., Mathur A., and Schiffman L.G., (1998), "Opportunities for Marketing Travel Services to New-Age Elderly", The Journal of Services Marketing, Vol. 12, No. 4, pp. 265-277.

14. The Ecotourism Society (1998), "Ecotourism Statistical Fact Sheet. www.ecotourism.org/datafr/html

15. Walkefield K.L. and Bush V.D. (1998), "Promoting Leisure Services: Economic and Emotional Aspects of Consumer Response", The Journal of Services Marketing, Vol. 12, No. 3, pp. 209-222.

16. Witt S. F. and Witt C.A. (1995), "Forecasting Tourism Demand: A Review of Empirical Research", International Journal of Forecasting 11, pp. 447-475.

SECTION
C

11

HUMAN RESOURCE DEVELOPMENT IN TOURISM INDUSTRY

S HUSAIN ASHRAF*
POOJA MATHUR**

INTRODUCTION

The tourism universe has been growing at a phenomenal rate for the last five decades especially after the Second World War and is positioned to go further at least in the coming two decades or so. The number of tourists worldwide are anticipated to be doubled approximately to one billion. This is going to mean **inherent** challenges of the system on both supply and demand fronts like increasing burden on people who plan, design, develop, manage, promote and protect tourism resources or train manpower. Moreover, external challenges will also surface like consumer will

* Reader, Department of Commerce, AMU, Aligarh.
** Research Scholar, Department of Commerce, AMU, Aligarh.

become increasingly discriminatory, more experienced and value conscious, consequently it will press the supplier to raise quality of services and to add value.

Therefore, the tourism industry has achieved new dimensions with travellers coming from near and far, to experience the intensity of India. With the roots of globalisation firmly in place in India, the tourism industry has started playing its role in generating growth and increasing awareness as well as securing to protect the country's invaluable resources. Developing nations are viewing tourism from a broader perspective in terms of its full impact on their regions and are playing an increasingly larger role in tourism planning. Tourism is not only an economic activity of importance to nation's development, but also an important medium of cultural exchanges among nations of the world. (e.g. Indo-German cultural programme, Indo-Russian exchange programme, Indo-Japan, etc.)

In the scenario of globalisation, competition among global players of tourism related service industries is unavoidable. Again, the global village concept considerably increased the expectation of people from all spheres. In such a situation only organisations capable of creating a competitive edge can continue their achievement. The apt way to reach such competitive edge in field is through human resource development. HRD is fast becoming a new competitive factor for tourism industry. Human Resource role is essentially an enabling role to provide the right context in which human performance occurs and the industry reaches its stated objectives. Therefore, enhancing international tourism with a similar large rise in domestic tourism demand, will place excessive pressure on countries' and operators' capabilities to provide sufficient personnel – educated and trained to the appropriate standard – for the range of tourism, managerial and skilled occupations. Training programmes to produce the necessary skilled staff is a challenge for all, while basic education to prepare its people to be trained for tourism is a priority in developing countries.

Thus, to succeed and counter the challenges, a full professional approach on the part of both destinations and travel trade is of paramount importance. A vital part of this professionalism is the ability to achieve properly planned tourism based on a comprehensive understanding of demand evolution and of development mechanisms. Therefore, the growth and development of the HR professional will have to focus on an understanding of the total management function, both in content and process. He must educate himself more adequately on the financial, marketing and the technical side of the industry operations and understand the strategic corporate process and the behaviour of the industry as a whole. He must consistently update himself in organisation behaviour, involve himself in organisational restructuring and initiate ideas for change. He must establish his role in the strategic management of the industry affairs and create a body of coherent and credible technology to support its strategic role in management. HR professionals must make adequate use of computer technology to the travel and tourism industry, which will further promote the relationship between vendor, intermediary and consumer. These developments will benefit, both, travel suppliers and travellers in the form of more efficient data handling and processing, reducing the requirement for staff and hence, lowering operating costs.

All these areas of focus indicate that the job of human resource professional in tourism industry will be a very demanding one and therefore a critical area of concern could be about where the people with the right quality are to be found. The profession has to do a lot to raise its standards, to get higher quality people into it and ensure that its members are educated generally in tourism industry as well as specifically in HRM to develop competent professionals to whom line experience as well as personnel experience would have to be imparted. This places a responsibility on those at the top of the profession, and those concerned with education and career planning of HR managers to ensure that aspiring HR professionals acquire the knowledge and competencies to act as performance managers as well as HRM specialists.

AIM & PHILOSOPHY OF HRD

HRD is a subject of national importance, having great relevance in a developing populous country like India. "Human resource" is the most crucial and difficult resource to tackle. The coming years, therefore, are the challenging years for HRD professionals. Efforts in introspection, recharging and building new bases would occupy the centre stage in the strategy formulation and implementation. The main aim and philosophy of HRD is to develop the workers or people enabling capacities by developing an environment which provides some amount of initiative, trust, openness, risk and commitment to work not just for the needs of tomorrow but even for those of the days after. The HRD philosophy believes that it is the responsibility of the top level manager to create a climate of development and trust so that people may give their best with a sense of satisfaction and growth. It assumes that the organisation will take care of their basic needs through a series of welfare measures and higher order needs through appropriate management styles and systems. Therefore the HRD programmes can reduce the consciousness gap between managers, supervisors and the masses of people, by training and development of workers because the success of any development programme depends upon a number of variables of which training is an important factor. Training, education and development of HRD provide the needed stimuli to initiate an impulse of change in the organisational apparatus and lead to improved efficiency, productivity and administrative performance.

Therefore, for the purpose of competing with globalised world, the perspectives of HRD in the future are not only educating people but broadly integrating the individual objectives with the strategic business plan and organisational objectives. Therefore, planning for development aims at increasing the ability of the individuals and groups to contribute to organisational effectiveness. Development programmes are designed to educate employees beyond the requirements of their present position so that they will be prepared for future promotions and be able take a broader view of their role in the organisation. This improved capability makes a person sharper in his job. Thus, HRD is an important component of any organisation and the organisation can develop, change and excel only if it possesses developed human resources.

EMERGING HRD DIMENSIONS

Liberalisation, globalisation and the transnational invasion ensure that managing organisational excellence would never be the same again. Due to the information technology explosion, increased global competition, rapidly changing market and deregulation, organisations are struggling for their survival and growth. The organisations have to redesign their outlook toward HRM, in fact, many of them have started to feel the chill blasts of domestic as well as international competition. They are beginning to realise that the winners in a borderless economy would be those that make best use of the experience, creativity from geographical diversity and honest professionalism of workers. Success would come to those who would manage to combine the virtue of conflicting paradigms rather than relying exclusively on a single set of pre-ordained theoretically right policies. In the light of these facts the HRM Practitioner and experts have to assume new and innovative roles and this would be possible when all the structures, systems and techniques that an organisation uses to help its employees to acquire and strengthen their capabilities are viewed under HRD technology.

The technological changes are forcing organisations to adopt new structures and to adopt to the environment. The obsolescence of certain jobs in the future will make it necessary for organisations to prepare workers with new skills and attitudes to cope with changes. One of the thrust areas of HRD function in future would be the creation of the type of organisational environment that will help to make work more satisfying to the employees so that the HRD managers may reduce the feeling of alienation, hostility and aggressive approach of their employees towards their jobs and superiors. Managing personnel would require sensitivity to the complex and changing values, aspirations and attitudes that the people bring to the workplace. Narrow specialisation was the hallmark of the organisation so far which has been replaced by multi-skill work process and that too is also giving way gradually to poly-dimensional organisational practices where the boundaries of section, department and division are shrinking and poly-dimensional corporate function is emerging. In order to contain the ever-emerging challenges, the future HRD functionaries will have to concentrate on a new basic thrust area within the organisation, offloading many of their functions to outside specialised agencies. The employees will require to have full perspective of the organisation. Hence·there will be demand for increasing precise communication system. More clarification of roles, goals and job responsibilities will be required which means active involvement of line managers to act as mentor and coach to stimulate, motivate and engage workers. Involvement of the line managers would be important in all HRD functions right from selection. For the survival and growth of the organisation "Quality" is the most important factor that will further increase with the coming of the competitive world market concept.

Emphasis on a quality movement, Total Quality Management, quality control, etc, will increase in the organisation and HRD functionaries have to provide the lead.

Thus, the HRD professionals have to undergo a complete change in attitude, working system, human relation skills, etc. There will be more concern for innovations and strategies. There will be no place for the ill prepared, the indolent and subservient staffer. But there will be more opportunities for the well trained, imaginative, innovative, up-to-date and aggressive professionals with broader and all comprehensive view of things.

Human Resource Development in Tourism in India

Public Sector

Public sector is playing a major role in HRD in India tourism. Following are the recommendations of Jha committee, which emphasised that public sector assume an active and positive role in promoting tourism. In 1965, Department of Tourism, Government of India, set-up three separate corporations, viz., Hotel Corporation of India Ltd., Indian Tourism Corporation Ltd. and India Tourism Transport Undertaking Ltd. These corporations were set up under the Provision of the Companies Act 1956. The main function of these corporations was to construct and manage hotels in the public sector, produce material for tourist publicity and to provide transport facilities to the tourists.

The Government later decided to merge these undertakings into one composite undertaking for the purpose of securing coordination in the policy and for the efficient and economic working of these corporations. Accordingly, in Oct. 1966 the Government set up a public sector undertaking, namely, the Indian Tourism by amalgamating the erstwhile three separate corporations which came into being with effect from March 1970.

Broadly, the objective and functions of the unified ITDC fall under the following categories:

1) Construction and management of hotels, motels, restaurants, guest houses and beach resorts at various places for accommodating tourists.

2) Provision of transport facilities to tourists.

3) Provision of entertainment facilities to tourists by way of organising cultural shows, music concerts, sound and light shows, etc.

4) Provision of publicity services to assist India's promotion overseas as a tourist destination and projecting the national importance of tourism at home.

With these objectives, ITDC has provided a wide range of services essential for the promotion of tourism.

Harnessing Human Resource

Manpower development has been a major concern for the Department of Tourism. A comprehensive effort has been launched to harness manpower resources adequately to meet the needs of fast expanding tourism industry. In the very specialised hotel catering sector, as well as in the larger area of management services relating to leisure management, tour operation, transportation and interpretation services, the Department of Tourism has launched ongoing programmes offering courses, workshops, seminars and conferences. Several public sector organisations and Government institutions are catering to these needs, some of which are as follows:

1) **ITDC:** ITDC has laid great emphasis on Human Resource Development Division during the year 1995-96. ITDC has a full fledged HRD centre which runs programmes for manpower development for employees' benefit. The Manpower Development Centre also conducted in-house

training programmes and trained executives & non-executives laying stress on quality management.

2) *Indian Institute of Tourism Travel Management*: The Indian Institute of Tourism Travel Management, founded by the Ministry of Tourism, is providing academic opportunities to graduates directly and in collaboration with universities for creating successful professionals in various fields. Programmes have ranged from subjects like planning tourism travel and tourism management, computer technology and communication in tourism orientation courses for probationers of All India and central services, immigration officers, intensive foreign language training programmes for guides which are being held in important tourist centres like Bombay, Delhi, Bangalore, Calcutta, etc. in languages like Arabic, German, French, Russian, and Spanish.

3) *National Council for Hotel Management and Catering Technology*: Training programmes in the field of hotel management, catering and nutrition are being taken up at the four institutes in New Delhi, Bombay, Madras and Calcutta. The training given at these institutes is a blend of theory and practical training including a period of industrial apprenticeship. Practical training is being emphasised with a scheme of adoption of institutes by hotel groups having been introduced recently. National Council for Hotel Management and Catering Technology was set up with a view to coordinate more closely the academic activities of the institutes, to evolve a common standard of admission and examination and to frame academic programmes in close association with the industry. The National Council for Hotel Management and Catering Technology will give emphasis to research, manpower development training programmes, setting up of guidelines to establish proper training standards and to also go international in its reach in terms of extending training and advising on hotel education.

4) *National Institute of Water Sports:* The Institute runs a number of courses for the development of human resource required for adventure tourism. For example, Water Sports Centre Management envisages to develop human resources required for various water sports like yatching, canoeing, skiing. This institute provides skilled manpower for maintaining water sports equipment and training of adventure tourist, interested in water sports. Located in Goa and being the first one in Asia, it is expected to provide the best human resource for the promotion of water sports and adventure tourism.

Private Sector

The contribution of private sector in promotion of tourism in India is beyond any description. The investments made by private sector can be seen through the rising travel industry and hotel industry mushrooming around the country at major tourist destinations. The new economic policy initiated by the government in 1991 which opened the Indian economy to private sector through liberalisation has given enough importance to the role of private sector. The liberalisation policy of the government has envisaged investment by multinational corporations in setting up hotels of international standards promoting tourist arrivals to the country.

Apart from hotels and airlines sector, there was major growth in the travel agency sector also. To meet the demands of human resources to the private sector establishments, training institutes of high repute with foreign collaboration were established. Some of these are as follows:

a) *Skyline Business School:* Skyline Business School, India is an associate of Skyline College, UAE, one of the largest institutions of higher learning in UAE. The mission of Skyline Business School is to provide its students with the best professional career prospects in the emerging global market-place and to equip them to become effective business managers. It was founded in association with the Sharjah Airport Authority and Civil Aviation with the aim of responding innovatively and effectively to the new training and educational needs of the travel and hospitality industry as well as the services sector.

b) **SITA Academy:** Recognising the growing need of the travel industry for well trained professionals, SITA is conscious of the quality of human contact in this trade. To fulfil this vacuum and its commitment to the cause of the industry, the SITA Travel and Tourism Academy was set up in 1962 which organises specialised courses in the field of travel and tourism and also in ticketing. These courses will become the yardstick for the industry in times to come.

The tourism industry in India is significantly poised at a take-off state and perhaps for the first time an integrated tourism development programme has been initiated. At various levels, greater interaction has been created between private and public sector in the industry, a greater sense of cohesiveness exists between the various ministries of the government of India. A more need based strategy is required for implementation of tourism policies by the Ministry and its various officers, combined with this is the increasing awareness of tourism as an industry and as a source of foreign exchange earnings for the country.

Problems of Development

1) **Lack of well defined status:** Tourism is relatively a new industry. In fact, many people choose not to define it as an industry. The term 'travel trade' was more commonly used until thirty-five years ago. Tourism consists of a number of unconnected enterprises, and it is not easy to prepare a

syllabus for an integrated course of training. The training required for hotel crafts such as cooking, restaurant services, housekeeping, etc. is more identifiable and traditional which may explain why there are many hotel schools but hardly any institution for imparting training in tourism.

2) *Lack of proper training:* One of the important factors in developing professionalism in the business of tourism and travel agency operations is that of training. While there are a number of good institutions in Europe, North America and a few other countries for training in hotel crafts and management, unfortunately, institutional training in tourism is almost non-existent in India. There are faculties in universities for autonomous colleges in India which are designated for training in hotel management and tourism. But the tourism agencies are looking for trained personnel but they are just not available.

3) *Lack of continuity of National Tourism Organisation:* Another important factor in HRD is continuity. In highly developed countries like the United States, UK, Switzerland, Spain and others, National Tourism Organisation mainly acts as a catalyst and leads the way in promoting tourism. But in developing countries, governments are playing a more decisive role in the development of tourism. It is therefore, most essential that national tourism organisations should also build up professionalism. Unfortunately, in the official hierarchies of most developing counties, the head of the National Tourist Organisation does not enjoy a senior status. He is generally looking for promotion in other sectors of the government, hence appointments of Director of Tourism and other senior staff are often of short duration and subject to haphazard changes.

4) *Lack of proper attitude of management towards HRD programmes:* Management's attitude towards HRD in most

of the organisations is not encouraging. Most of them are under the impression that spending money on HRD for workers may not yield quantifiable returns. Generally, unlike an investment in a machine, investment in HRD is not seen as directly translating into returns. It is also felt that an educated worker may turn out to be a problem child. Their perception is that the workers are bound to work as they are paid wages, otherwise positive measures like suspensions can be used.

5) **Attitude of trade union:** Trade unions in India seem to respond cautiously to any HRD initiatives. Because of their distrust in the intention of management, they look at HRD as only a mechanism to brainwash the workers. Thus, they see a threat in the concept. Several union leaders feel that HRD could be the same old game of the employer of divide and rule. They also feel that once management is able to directly communicate with workers it is likely that the trade union's impact will be diluted.

6) **Lack of proper response from employees:** Workers sometimes reject the HRD programme meant for development especially when they perceive HRD programme as management manipulation in which workers are expected to learn new skills and contribute something for nothing. The workers believe that management is interested only in their output and not in their welfare. If such attitude is developed, it is difficult to get a worker into training programme.

7) **Management's misunderstanding of HRD techniques:** HRD for workers in some organisations have failed because management was unable to understand that HRD is a continuous activity and consequently they ceased their responsiveness to workers' suggestions after initial enthusiasm was over. Failure in many Indian companies is also because of incorrect understanding of the word 'voluntary' in the

definition of Quality circles – a prominent HRD technique. In India, we interpret the word 'voluntary' as implying "do it if you want to, leave it if you do not want to do it". Such understanding amounts to the failure of HRD efforts in India.

8) **Inefficiency:** Organisational inefficiency means its outputs are not in tune with the nature and extent of resources employed for the purpose. In other words, there is no optimum utilisation of human and physical resources of an organisation. The corporation is not result oriented, the limited resources being to use are not bringing the desirable output. An obvious example of this is ITDC. All the above cited points like limited resources, employee dissatisfaction and mismanagement should be held responsible for the overall inefficiency of the corporation. Lack of team spirit and dissatisfaction on the part of employees are factors responsible for their half-hearted services to the industry. Employees themselves accept the fact that there is lack of belongingness and responsibility. So most of the people remain indifferent to the overall performance of the industry.

SUGGESTIONS

1) It is high time that the Government, after reviewing the growing tourist arrivals and the socio- economic benefits of the tourism phenomenon, accord it the status of a priority sector. The Government should also ensure more resource allocation for the overall development of this sector.

2) In view of the growing trends in the industry and the need for human resources, the Government should set up an Expert Committee comprising of human resource development professionals, people from the tourism industry, prominent economists and intellectuals to study and assess

various aspects of HRD and come out with a national policy on HRD in the tourism sector.

3) Tourism being a highly labour intensive industry, there should be an integrated HRD system with both public and private sector participation to develop human resources to meet the requirements of the industry.

4) To maintain international standards, manpower resource division of public and private sector organisations should see that HRD programmes are conducted with foreign collaborations.

5) In this era of modernisation, the planners should ensure the best advanced technologies are exposed to the personnel for maximum efficiency and customer satisfaction.

6) There should be a performance appraisal system for the employee incorporating self-appraisal and a review of his performance in relation to objectives and other behaviours. Along with this, there should be a potential appraisal system to make thorough potential appraisals of the employee annually.

7) For the upgradation of human resource, there should be a career development and career planning mechanism to make the employees aware of the general phases of their development.

8) The training establishments should have foreign exchange programmes (personnel) to ensure quality training in successive development of human resource.

9) Zonal manpower resource centre should be formed to recognise tourism as a factor for regional development. These manpower resource development centres should conduct studies on the availability of skilled and semi-skilled human resources in their respective regions.

10) To study about the various training establishments and training programmes conducted by different countries, the planners should send study missions for information which will be useful in formulating plans and strategies for HRD and setting up training establishments in India.

11) To churn out the best human resources from various educational institutions including universities. There is a need to incorporate vocational training programmes to create human resource from the grass roots level. There should be awareness programmes and career orientation lectures to encourage youth to opt for careers in the different segments of the tourism industry.

12) A parliamentary affairs committee should look into introducing education reforms bill to ensure quality education with an industrial approach. This will, in turn, develop human resources to a large extent.

13) HRD programmes should give due stress to high technology functional training to impart necessary skills.

14) Seminars, workshops should be conducted to discuss problems and prospects of HRD at the national and international level.

15) For awareness and the implementation of various HRD schemes there should be a confederation of Indian Travel Industries (CITI). The CITI can monitor the implementation and advise the Government in policy formulations for the development of the Tourism Industry at large and HRD in particular.

CONCLUSION

"Human Resources Development" is increasingly gaining attention from human resource specialists, academicians and employees alike. The importance of HRD will undoubtedly increase further. There is likely to be a knowledge exploration in HRD in the next decade. According to WTO forecast, tourism growth prospects for India are very bright and tourist arrivals and receipts are likely to increase during the coming years. With these growing trends in the tourism industry in India which is labour intensive industry or a 'people industry', HR plays an important role in managing, operating, planning and promoting tourism industry. Therefore, HRD efforts in tourism industry require a major transformation in the attitudes, behaviours and values of employees and management. This can be possible if appropriate conditions are provided by the organisation to make HRD successful and introduce it as a total system within the industry.

Thus, HRD has a major role to play for the development of this sector. HRD should be taken on a priority basis and adequate planning measures should be done accordingly because efficient human resources can increase customer satisfaction, and create a competitive edge in this globalised world.

REFERENCES

1. Rao, T.V. and Pereira, D.F. *Recent Experiences in HRD*, New Delhi, Oxford and IBM, 1986.

2. Rao, T.V. *Planning for Human Resources Development*, VIKLPA (IIMA). July – Sept. 87.

3. Percy K. Singh, *Fifty Years of Indian Tourism*, Kanishka Publishers, New Delhi.

4. Ratandeep Singh, *Infrastructure of Tourism in India*, Kanishka Publishers, New Delhi.

5. Arun Kumar Sarkar, *Action Plan and Priorities in Tourism Development*, Kanishka Publishers, New Delhi.

6. A.K. Bhatia, *Tourism in India - History & Development*, New Delhi Sterling.

7. Krishan K. Karma, *Tourism Theory, Planning and Practice*, Indus Publishing Company, New Delhi.

8. Rakesh Kapoor, *Tourism Policy Organisation and Management*, Kanishka Publisher, New Delhi.

TRAVEL AGENCY HRD PRACTICES: AN INVESTIGATION

MOHINDER CHAND*
VINAY CHAUHAN**

INTRODUCTION

Today, the travel industry is becoming more and more competitive. The travel agency business is no longer in amateurism. Over the last two decades, the travel companies have transformed their pattern and structure to meet tough challenges in the international tourism market. Obviously, in this volatile business environment, only a successful travel/tour company will change to meet competitive threats and opportunities to match the needs of a new travel market, and will bring flexibility, creativity,

---

* Assistant Prof., Dept. of Tourism: Kurukshetra University, Kurukshetra.
** Research Scholar, Dept. of Tourism, Kurukshetra University, Kurukshetra.

innovation, determination and professionalism into its operations (M. Chand 2000).

Travel agency/tour operator employment within tourism industry is a visible and relatively popular option for tourism graduates and postgraduates. It is also a prominent option for those individuals who wish to accept challenging careers and are prepared to devote considerable energy and enthusiasm to their job. Travel/tour companies need tourism professionals specialising in different operational and managerial functions – tour planning and research, travel information, destination services, ticketing and reservation, marketing and sales, finance and accounts, conferences and conventions and so forth. Therefore, company's recruitment policy may be not only to focus on functional expertise but on attitudes and approaches that fit their corporate goals and culture. Unfortunately, the employee turnover is very high in tourism industry – especially in travel agencies and tour operation business. There ought to be some obvious reasons – conventional approach to 'HR practices'. So far there is no evidence that any kind of 'HRD' approach is being followed by the travel agencies. Even the travel agency literature is silent in this context. However, some recent studies have been conducted to highlight the significance of HR practices in hotel companies. For example, both Lucas (1995, 1996) and Price (1994) find personnel specialists to be more in evidence in the hotel and catering sector than elsewhere. Harrington and Abehurst (1996) also observed that hotels are taking HR practices more seriously. They are adopting modern HR techniques to train and develop employees. Thus, the earlier studies have looked at travel companies in isolation and have inferred from the result that the industry is lagging in terms of professionalism. Taking into consideration this paradoxical situation, the present study has been conducted to examine the HRD practices adopted by travel/tour companies.

Objectives

The main objectives of the study are:

▶ To identify the main issues related to human resources in travel/tour companies;

▶ To study the existing HRD policies and practices adopted by the travel/tour companies; and

▶ To suggest 'ways and means' by which travel/tour companies can prepare themselves for the 21ˢᵗ century and beyond.

Hypothesis

The following hypothesis were tested:

1. The top management does not actively support HRD practices.

2. There is no formal recruitment and selection system.

3. Training and development is not significant at all levels.

With a view to design effective and extensive questionnaire, the authors conducted a pilot survey (though e-mail and personal visit) to identify the main HR issues in travel/tour companies. This process evolved the following HR problems as being of crucial significance to the future of the travel/tour companies:

▶ Lack of proper manpower policies;

▶ Improperly designed recruitment/selection policies;

▶ Ineffective managerial and professional level training;

▶ Lack of interface/coordination between tourism, educational institutions and travel agencies/tour operations;

▶ Limited opportunities for career advancement;

▶ Low pay package as compared to other industries;

▶ Unhealthy growth of small scale travel agencies (unrecognised);

▶ Unable to develop a culture that attracts quality people to the agency; and

▶ Insufficient emphasis on service-delivery/customer-relationship aspect.

Sample Design

In April 2000, a structured questionnaire entitled "Travel Agency HRD Practices: An Investigation" was distributed personally and through e-mail to HRD managers and HRD departments. The sampling method was judgmental and consisted of 86 travel/ tour companies. The sample was designed in such a manner that it would give an appropriate representation to the various travel companies. However, while selecting the sample companies, due consideration was given to national award winner organisations, of both small and big size. Of the 86 companies approached, 49 (56.96 per cent) agreed to participate in the survey and returned the completed questionnaires.

Research Instrument

The study was conducted via a written questionnaire consisting of 25 questions divided into two categories:

▶ Company profiles (5 questions).

▶ HRD practices (20 questions).

The survey obtained detailed information on existing HRD policies and practices. The participants in this study were asked to rate the importance of each of the 20 HRD attributes on a multi-scale pattern. The percentage analysis was used to ascertain whether any of the sought HRD attributes were more widely reported in any travel/ tour company.

Results and Discussion

Responses were received from 86 travel/tour companies, only 49 travel agencies (57 per cent) participated in the survey and returned the completed questionnaire. Fortunately, this was achieved through reminders and number of telephone calls, prior to which the response rate was 45.2 per cent.

The questionnaire responses were analysed and examined by percentage of each variable/ attributes included in the survey. To perform the first part of this analysis, the most important characteristics identified for each travel/tour company were:

▶ Survey respondents employed an average of 95 employees.

▶ 80 per cent respondents had multi-area of operation: inbound, outbound and domestic tourism.

▶ 36 per cent travel/tour companies had one product line, namely general tour, while 64 per cent travel/tour companies had multi-product line, i.e., business tours, general tours, FIT, adventure tours etc.

Table 1 depicts that there is an evidence to suggest the reported usage of HRD practices by travel/tour companies within the sample.

TABLE 1: USAGE OF HRD POLICIES/ PRACTICES AND STRATEGIES IN TRAVEL/ TOUR COMPANIES

		N-49 (Percentage)	Valid cases
1.1	Separate HRD Department	47.55	38
1.2	HRD function performed	85.00	42
1.3	Time spent on HR matters	70.73	41
1.4	Professionally qualified personnel in HRD dept.	79.49	39
1.5	Manpower planning	93.02	43
1.6	Categories of people recruited	86.49	37
1.7	Organisation culture offered	81.39	43
1.8	Degree of difficulty experienced in filling job vacancies	95.74	47

Contd...

1.9	Skill deficiencies in jobs	91.67	48
1.10	Selection of tourism management students	51.43	35
1.11	Preference of external recruitment methods	85.71	42
1.12	Psychographic test as the norm for selection	45.56	36
1.13	Significance of training and development at all levels	93.75	48
1.14	Training techniques adopted	74.36	39
1.15	Overall effectiveness of external training & development programmes	55.00	40
1.16	Overall effectiveness of in-house training & development programmes	85.00	40
1.17	A merit element in the pay of staff	89.58	48
1.18	Performance appraisal methods used at all levels	93.75	48
1.19	HR strategy/policies deliberately integrated with corporate goals	78.26	46
1.20	HRD policies and practices proposed by top mgt.	84.44	45

Firstly, looking at the point of separate HRD department, only 47.55 per cent respondents agreed that they had separate HRD department where as 85 per cent respondents said that the HRD activities were performed by the top management either by MD or GM. It would seem to indicate that personnel specialists within sample organisations were to some extent qualified and spent an average of 70.73 per cent time on HRs matters. The analysis indicated that 93 per cent travel companies had proper manpower planning concentrating on personnel having professional qualification such as MTM/MTA or PGD in tourism management, etc. Incidentally, a majority of travel companies were not dependent on campus recruitment but were recruiting their employees through direct method. In this way they were giving more preference to external recruitment method (85.71 per cent). Thus, looking at recruitment and selection, trainability was more frequently cited as a major selection criteria. Formal system for communicating the organisational culture to new staff was also found more in evidence in travel agencies. However, only 45 per cent of the travel agency sample claims to use psychological tests as a norm for selection of staff.

The survey asked HRD managers to indicate the degree of difficulty they had experienced in filling job vacancies – managerial, professional, trained and untrained – over the last 12-15 months. As can be seen from Table 2, though HRD managers were divided in their opinions regarding the difficulty of recruiting for trained positions, they reported significant difficulties in recruiting qualified managerial and professionals. Only minor difficulties were being experienced in filling untrained positions.

TABLE 2: DEGREE OF DIFFICULTY IN FILLING JOB VACCINES AT VARIOUS LEVELS

	Serious (%)	Moderate (%)	Minor (%)
Managerial	51.79	35.93	8.18
Professional	47.12	38.66	8.81
Trained	41.90	28.1	20.76
Untrained	2.0	5.1	9.36

Table 3 lists the skill deficiencies identified in the study. Respondents agreed that managers had some mild deficiencies in tourism conceptual knowledge, problem solving and foreign languages, whereas in professional employees had serious deficiencies in problem solving and mild deficiencies in finance, leadership and conceptual knowledge. However, in other personnel, critical deficiencies in general attitude, foreign languages and in many other areas were reported.

TABLE 3: SKILL DEFICIENCIES IN VARIOUS JOB CATEGORIES

Skills	Managers	Professionals	Other Personnel
▶ General attitude			C
▶ Tourism conceptual knowledge	M	M	S C
▶ Travel agency/tour operation function & activities	-	-	C
▶ Operational areas			
– Marketing			S

Contd...

– HRD			C
– Finance	M	M	C
– Product development			C
▶ Leadership	M	-	S
▶ Problem solving	M	S	S
▶ Foreign languages	M	M	C
▶ Knowledge of modern technology	M	M	C

Note: C = Critical Deficiency
      S = Serious Deficiency
      M = Mild Deficiency

In one policy area, namely training and development, ninety four per cent HRD managers agreed that training and development is significant at all levels. However, there were divergent opinions among the HRD managers regarding the training and development approaches. A significant proportion of respondents supported the concept of behavioural and functional training and development. A relatively high proportion of HRD managers (Table 1) thought that existing external training and development programmes are not very effective in preparing managers, professionals and other employees. 85 per cent HRD managers, however, rated the effectiveness of internal/in-house training and development programmes significantly higher than the external programmes. Further, the investigation revealed that most of the travel/tour companies are focusing on improving the customer service skills of their managers and trained personnel.

Concerning pay package, 89.93 per cent travel agencies used merit pay system. 75 per cent HRD managers agreed that their company's package ensures maximum employee benefit. However, 47 per cent HRD managers agreed that their company's package is in line with the best in the industry. Performance appraisal is used in maximum travel agencies. Respondents uniformly recognised this crucial HRD function as an area of grave concern to them. This is the area where the largest dissonance between HRD managers and MD or GM emerged. However, an average

96 per cent HRD managers reported that there is formal appraisal system in their organisation. Naturally, a formal appraisal can either serve as an evaluative mechanism to determine merit pay awards, or for the purpose of overall development.

To assess the extent to which HR policies/ strategies are integrated with corporate goals/strategy, a question was asked from the respondents. The analysis indicated that 78.26 per cent respondents reported the existence of HR strategy, being formally and actively supported by senior management. The importance accorded to HR issues is further reflected by the fact that the travel agencies are more likely to have a mission statement. Further, these companies claimed to have achieved an integration between their HR policy and their business strategy.

CONCLUSION AND TENTATIVE RECOMMENDATIONS

Most HRD managers agreed that service quality is the number one factor that contributes to the success or failure of a travel agency. In fact, quality of service is directly related to employee's performance. Thus, a travel/tour company has no choice as between 'HRD or Non-HRD'. The only choice is to adopt HRD practices that will make it different from its competitors.

The results reported within this investigation lend support to the growing level of interest in HRD especially in large scale travel/tour companies. The analysis indicates that 93 per cent travel companies have proper manpower planning. However, these are not rigid to professional qualification criteria for selection of employees. Most of the respondents are in favour of removing the skill deficiencies prevailing at various levels. Seventy eight per cent HRD managers reported the existence of formal HR strategy. Further, the analysis demonstrates that both large and medium scale travel companies have taken bold steps to improve and develop their HRD policies and practices. However, there is a need to create/develop learning organisation culture to yield the result of HRD practices.

Tentative Recommendations

▶ Travel/Tour companies should increase the budget outlay assigned to HRD activities;

▶ HRD objectives should be properly defined;

▶ Manpower planning should focus on all levels;

▶ Choose recruitment team carefully;

▶ Build ownership into pay package;

▶ Travel companies should incorporate performance based career growth;

▶ Maintain cordial relationship with universities and institutions offering tourism management courses; and finally

▶ Travel companies must strive to improve the levels of their employees' skills in the area of information technology, marketing, conceptual knowledge of tourism and customer service relationship to survive in the 21ˢᵗ century and beyond.

REFERENCES

Chand, Mohinder, *Travel Agency Management - An Introductory Text*, Anmol Publications Pvt. Ltd., New Delhi, 2000.

Harrington, D. and Akehurt, G., (1966), "*Service Quality and Business Performance in the UK Hotel Industry*", International Journal of Hospitality Management, Vol. 15, No. 3, pp. 282-298.

Lucas, R. (1995), *Managing Employee Relations in the Hotel and Catering Industry*, London Cassell.

Lucas, R. (1996), "*Industrial Relations in Hotel and Catering, Neglect and Paradox?*" British Journal of Industrial Relations, Vol, 34, No. 2, pp. 267-286.

Price, L. (1994), *"Poor Personnel Practice in Hotel and Catering Industry: Does it Matter?"* Human Resource Management Journal, Vol, 4, No.4, pp. 44-62.

Pareek, V. and Sasodia, V. (Ed.), *HRD in the New Millennium*, Tata McGraw Hill, New Delhi, 1999.

David, M., Paul, B. and Jennifer, M. *"Human Resource Development,"* Crest Publishing House, New Delhi, 2001.

ESSENTIALS FOR EXCELLENCE IN PROFESSIONALS IN THE TOURISM INDUSTRY

M M GOEL

It hardly needs any justification that the tourism industry plays an important role in the development of an economy. To realise the full potential of tourism as a foreign exchange earner as well as a human resource development (HRD) activity, we need sincere, dedicated and enthusiastic manpower. In this paper, an attempt has been made to identify the various attributes required for tourism industry professionals, we study this aspect the SHE model of women empowerment. Women can play a much greater role in tourism industry by harnessing their feminine strengths in communication, relationship building and conflict management. Being a woman, she possesses the bearing and rearing capacity of a child (genetically not a man's capacity). She is more caring

* Reader in Economics & Former Chairman, Deptt. of Journalism, Kurukshetra University, Kurukshetra (India).

being a daughter, sister, wife, mother in personal life and also in professional life of any occupation. Motherhood is truly a recognised skill, required in tourism industry of today and tomorrow. The female managerial style boosts productivity & could circumvent the usual symptoms of professional high altitude sicknesses. She manages both a family and a career and is a professional asset, not a liability, because she knows all about cool multitasking in pressure cooker environments. As tourism professionals, women have a gender advantage as the 'e' in e-commerce also begins to stand for emotions making the tourism industry become more touchy-feely. Truly, women professionals can look after various issues in tourism industry with a sensitive perspective and in a better way.

To develop appropriate and suitable manpower for the tourism industry, we need to provide them suitable training in all aspects of HRD. Sincerity, dedication and enthusiasm of the manpower of the tourism industry of view of the changing economic scenario of liberalisation, privatisation, and globalisation (LPG) is the need of the day, for which I would like to justify feminisation of tourism industry, through the 'SHE' model given below:

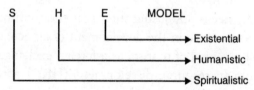

To survive, sustain and develop in the 21st century, the tourism professional needs to be made existential through Retention, Respect and Responsibility (3R of Human Resource Management). Women manpower is more existential because of her higher emotional quotient (e.q.) including patience, motivating herself, motivating others and empathising with others in all circumstances. Further, to make tourism professionals existential I have developed 'ASK' model of existence given below:

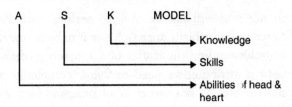

According to ASK model of existence, the tourism manpower must have complete, overall up-to-date, accurate knowledge o the profession. Skill of writing tourist accounts is not an easy task and is a science as well as an art. It is worth quoting Alexander Pope

"True ease in writing come by art not by chance

As s(he) moves easiest who has learnt to dance."

The skill of writing can certainly be developed through a lot of reading. It needs to be noted that societies and nations can live without writing but no society can exist without reading. Further, we need the skill of operating computer in the modern era of information technology, which calls for MCA model given below:

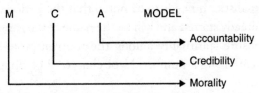

According to MCA model, the tourism manpower needs to be self-accountable and must establish credibility through ethics of morality. The last (but not the least) attribute of ASK model of existence is the abilities of head and heart to form the positive attitude for becoming existential in the profession through enthusiastic endeavour with patience, confidence and intelligence.

The second important component of the SHE model to make tourism manpower is Humanistic. Without begin humanistic, we can not and will not be able to perform our duties properly. Therefore, humanistic approach needs to be accepted as a panacea for understanding the duties of a tourism professional. For this essential attribute, we need to follow completely and absolutely sloka number 15 of chapter 17 of Bhagwad Gita given below:

"Anudvega- karan vakyam satyam priyahitam ca yat
Svadhyayabhyasanam caiva van-mayam tapa ucyate"

(B.G.: 17:15)

"Words that neither hurt nor provoke,
Truthfully to benefit others are spokes,
Or in process of self study pronounced,
O Arjun, to penance of speech amount."

Meaning thereby, meditative communion with one's own true self and uttering words that cause no agitation and that are truthful, pleasant and beneficial are called the austerity of speech. Thus, the tourism manpower needs to be objective and dependable to know or to tell the truth by becoming humanistic.

The third and final attribute of the SHE model is spiritualistic. It needs to be noted that the period of consciousness has already started and will be the name of the game in 21st century. To ensure spirituality among the tourism professionals we have advocated sloka number 22 of chapter 9 of Bhagwad Gita given below:

"ananyas cintayanto mam janah paryupasate
tesam nityabhiyuktanam yoga – ksemam vahamy aham"

(B.G.: 9:22)

"Who set their minds on one supreme?
And make me their worship theme,
As yogies of equanimity well qualify,
I aid them and there needs supply."

Meaning thereby, those who always worship me with exclusive devotion, meditating on my transcendental form to them

I carry what they lack, and I preserve what they have. In fact, spiritually guided materialism needs to be understood and propagated and calls for moving from wants based economy to needs based economy. Spirituality is essential for the removal of stress and strain as well as the social and economic health of the society for all times to come.

Thus, it needs to be emphasised that gender sensitisation can be taken care appropriately only through feminisation of tourism industry through the SHE model. Tourism industry can be consumer friendly and socially beneficial only if undertaken in accordance with NAW approach. Here, NAW stands for Need, Affordability and Worth of the services. The pertinent questions to be put before the tourist are:

▶ Does s(he) need the service, which has been so glamorously advertised?

▶ Is the service affordable?

▶ Is the service worth its price?

It needs to be pointed out that the services of the tourism industry would be popular only if they satisfy the essential need of the tourists (foreign as well as domestic) and are utilitarian. Glamour alone cannot be a substitute for the basic requirement of need, affordability and worth (NAW) of the services. To remove crime and corruption in tourism industry, we need to practise the zero tolerance concept of the worthy Prime Minister. Of course, there is a strong case for insurance policy for all those who accept and adopt zero tolerance against crime and corruption as a challenge. It is firmly believed by the author that by removing the crime and corruption prevailing in the tourism industry, we can increase its contribution to Gross National Product by at least one per cent. Good governance in tourism industry can create heaven for honest and hell for the corrupt and criminal. This shall lead to good health of tourism which is heaven for the soul of the tourists and hell for their diseases. The moral values imbibed in the manpower of tourism industry are capable of making tourism a corruption free activity.

To adopt and accept the normative approach to HRD in tourism industry, it is essential to understand SIMPLE model of HRD (developed by the author elsewhere) consisting of following human development activities, namely Spiritual development, Intuition development, Mental level development, Love your self attitude development and Emotional quotient (EQ) development. The synergy of these aspects of HRD is an essential requirement for professionals in the tourism industry to emerge and realise their full potential.

To sum up, I wish to emphasise that for every ill of tourism industry in 21st century, there are Vedic pills and Bhagwad Gita is the panacea. To create tourism culture in India and elsewhere in the world there is need of converting holiday culture into holy day culture.

REFERENCES

1.	A.C. Bhaktivedanta Swami Prabupada: *Bhagwad Gita – As it is*, The Bhaktivedanta Book Trust, Bombay, 1983.

2.	M.M. Goel, *Implications of Bhagvad Gita for Sustainable Human Development*, Samarika by Gita Kendra Kurukshtra Development Board, 1999.

3.	M.M. Goel, *Feminisation of Media and Advertising, Media Newsense*, September 2000.

4.	M.M. Goel, *Lessons from Bhagvad Gita for Banking Industry*, Economic Dateline, September 2001.

SECTION

D

CHAPTER

14

KAPAL MOCHAN FAIR – A THRUST TO PILGRIMAGE TOURISM IN HARYANA

ADARSH BATRA*

INTRODUCTION

The evolution of tourism could be attributed as journey undertaken since ancient times for religious motives to places accepted as being sacred. Such pilgrimages provided strong reason to travel, either singly or in groups, for the purpose of spiritual benefit.

India is witnessing a curious phenomenon: vacationers are no longer driven by sun, surf, sand and snow, but are instead rushing towards places of worship. Especially in India, the pull of religious tourism is stronger than holiday tourism. It is being

* Lecturer, Tourism & Travel Management, M.L.N. College, Yamuna Nagar.

observed that increase in pilgrim traffic is not only a result of the increase in middle class affluence, but also due to better travel facilities and conveniences available at places of worship. Pilgrimages accelerate the development of roads, transportation and accommodation facilities and, in turn, increasing numbers of people undertake journeys, thereby providing a strong motivation for the faithful.

KAPAL MOCHAN FAIR

Haryana is known as the cradle of Indian civilisation. The famous law book of Manu connoted Haryana as Brahma Warta where the religious and social system grew up and spread to the rest of the country. Yamuna Nagar is also a part of this holy land and Bilaspur is full of ancient and historical places.

About five lakh pilgrims from Haryana, Himachal Pradesh, Uttar Pradesh, Rajasthan and other states visit the annual Kapal Mochan Mela which is held at Bilaspur, 20 km from Yamuna Nagar, the district headquarters of the state of Haryana. That makes the distance from Kurukshetra 70 km (Yamuna Nagar to Kurukshetra – 50 kms). Bilaspur is said to be a distortion of the name Vyaspur, after the great sage Ved Vyas who wrote the Mahabharata.

The most famous pilgrimage in the area is Kapal Mochan or Rin Mochan where a big fair is held annually on Kartika Poornima, the full moon day of Kartik (November). The pilgrims have a holy dip in the sacred waters of Kapal Mochan, Rin Mochan and Suraj Kund in the early hours of Kartik Poornima and perform puja on the concluding day of the Mela. This fair has assumed significance in the sense that it has become a symbol of Hindu-Sikh unity and harmony. It is a fair celebrated by both the communities. Lakhs of people belonging to various communities assemble here for a holy dip in the Kapal Mochan tank.

The legend related to Kapal Mochan tank has been mentioned in the Mahabharata and the Puranas. Legend has it that Brahma, Vishnu and Mahesh had gathered here in the beginning of Kaliyuga to perform a yajna. Three "agnikunds" – "Surajkund", "Som srover" and "Rin Mochan" – were erected by Brahma for the yajna. This was objected to by Vishnu and Shiva. This enraged Brahma. He could not even recognise his daughter, Saraswati, and began harassing her. Saraswati ran to Shiva who chopped off one of Brahma's five heads. In turn, Shiva was cursed for this act and his body turned black. Shiva vainly visited many holy places to get rid of the curse. Finally, at Sindhu Vana, he overheard a conversation between a cow and its calf and learnt about a dip in "Som Sarover". The dip relieved him of the curse.

According to Skand Purana, three fire pits (agnikunds) were created by Brahma for performance of yajna. The fire pit in the north became known as Plakhch Tirth. It is located near Rampur about 6 km north of Kapal Mochan. The fire pit in the south became known as Somras Tirth. It was in the shape of half moon and later on became famous as Kapal Mochan. The third which was dose to Kapal Mochan was called Rin Mochan Tirth.

According to the legend, those who take bath in Kapal Mochan tank in the bright half of the Kartika month and visit the lingam of Lord Shiva situated at a little distance, get eternal bliss. A number of sculptures of Lord Shiva and Parvati and Ganesh of the 9th and 10th century AD have been found here.

According to the Mahabharata, five Pandavas performed puja at Kapal Mochan after the battle of Kurukshetra to relieve themselves of killing a Brahma, Dronacharya. They washed their weapons in the water of the "Rin Mochan" tank.

Towards the east of Kapal Mochan tank is a Gurdwara dedicated to Guru Gobind Singh. He is said to have stayed here for 52 days after the battle with the hilly rulers in AD 1682. He is also said to have cleaned the weapons used in the battle in Rin

Mochan tank and this place on the tank is called "Shastra Ghat" Guru Gobind Singh Ji. A stone slab at this gurudwara, which seems to be a lower part of some sculpture, has an inscription written in Brahmi script. The inscription goes back to 7th to 8th century AD.

ACCOMMODATION

Cheap accommodation in the form of Dharmshalas is made available by different religious and social institutions for the stay of pilgrims visiting this place. Among them Kamboj Dharmshala, Gujar Dharmshala, Kashyap Dharmshala, Jat Dharmshala, Ravidas Dharmshala, Saini Dharmshala, Brahma Dharmshala, Balmiki Temple and Moge Valon Ki Dharmshala are famous.

For the development of this religious and historic place, district administration has made the establishment of Kapal Mochan Trust in the Year 1988 of which the Deputy Commissioner of Yamuna Nagar is the chief patron. Apart from public officials, important personalities in the field of social service are also members of this trust. The collection is utilised on the renovation and development of this place.

Every year, one month before the commencement of the mela, District administration takes all necessary steps to make this mela a success. State Government usually sanctions handsome sum of about 5 to 6 lakhs every year. The tanks are thoroughly cleaned, repaired and filled with fresh water. On all the three tanks, separate bathing arrangement is made for women. The entire mela area is divided into different sectors under the control of the Magistrate. A good number of sodium, mercury lights and bulbs are installed to keep away darkness and to make overall atmosphere lively. Special transformers of different capacities (100 KV, 200 KV) are installed to regulate uninterrupted supply of electricity.

District administration mainly carries out the following tasks:

▶ To maintain law and order in the mela area, sufficient number of police personnel are deployed under the supervision of S.P. Yamuna Nagar. On all the four corners of mela entry point, metal detectors are deployed. A police control room is also established.

▶ To maintain cleanliness and hygienic conditions, C.M.O Yamuna Nagar supervises the area. Medical officers throw drugs (to make germ free) in the water of Sarover.

▶ Public Health Department carries out the task of providing temporary urinals and toilets. Block development officers and members of panchayat assist in these operations.

▶ Public Health Department provides fresh and clean water for drinking purpose in the mela area.

▶ P.W.D. oversees the condition of roads leading to mela area.

▶ G.M. Haryana Roadways, Yamuna Nagar makes adequate arrangement for a good frequency of buses leading to mela area as well as arrangement of providing crane to the mela area.

▶ District Food Supply Department makes arrangement for providing temporary shops to mela so that people can purchase rice, sugar, flour, kerosene oil at subsidised rates.

▶ For any vehicle entering mela area, nominal toll tax is charged by the Government, for:

Private Buses	-	Rs 30 per trip
Public Trucks/ Taxi	-	Rs 15 per trip
Motor Car/ Jeep	-	Rs 5 per trip
Auto Rickshaw/ Tanga	-	Rs 2 per trip
Scooter/ Motor Cycle	-	Rs 1 per trip

▶ P.R.O. Yamuna Nagar provides public address system to provide information from time to time.

▶ Emergency arrangement of boats and divers is made to avoid any mishappening.

Accessibility

For tourists visiting Kapal Mochan for pilgrimage purpose there are well built and maintained railways and roadways and roads in fine state. The name of the railway station is Jagadhri, famous for utensils all over India, at Yamuna Nagar. Haryana Roadways provides sufficient number of buses to transport pilgrims.

REFERENCES

1. R.N. Kaul, *Dynamics of Tourism*, Vol. 1, 1985.
2. Information available at the Office of Deputy Commissioner, Yamuna Nagar.
3. Information available at the Office of Supdt. of Police Jagadhur.

CHAPTER
15

PILGRIMAGE TOURISM
IN INDIA

RAJENDRA MISHRA*

Indian culture has emphasised the significance of pilgrimage for spiritual progress. Every Indian has an inner desire to go for pilgrimage at least once in his lifetime. The institution of pilgrimage to holy places is an ancient and continuing religious tradition of the Hindus. Many sacred places located in various parts of India attract a large number of pilgrims from within the country and outside the country. The spread of sacred places throughout India has created an essentially continuous religious space, which the otherwise great regional cultural diversity becomes less significant for the movement of pilgrims over long distances.

All major Indian scriptures – Rig Veda, Ramayana, Mahabharata, Puranas and Upanishadas are filled with the accounts of pilgrimages undertaken by the great sages and kings.

---

*   Senior Lecturer, Faculty of Management Studies, University of Jammu.

These may be quoted as oldest examples of pilgrimage tourism. The real contribution to pilgrimage tourism came from Shankaracharya. By establishing four dhamas in Puri, Dwarka, Badrinath and Sringeri, he has, as a matter of fact, become an initiator of pilgrimage tourism. Other sacred places of Hindu pilgrimage are Kurukshetra, Saptapuris, i.e. seven sacred cities, Ayodhya, Mathura, Haridwar, Varanasi, Kanchipuram, Ujjain and Dwarka; four places of Kumbh ka Mela Prayag, Haridwar, Ujjain and Nasik; twelve Jyotirlingas; fifty one 'Shakti-Pethas'; 108 major Vishnu temples; eight self-manifested holy places – Sri Rangam, Tirupati, Sri Mushanam, Thotadari, Shaligram, Pushkara, Naimisharanya and Badrinath. The Himalayas are considered a sacred mountain range. The seven most sacred rivers are – Ganga, Yamuna, Godavari, Saraswati, Narmada, Sindhu and Kaveri. All the three seas surrounding Indian peninsula are considered sacred.[1]

DEVELOPMENT OF PILGRIMAGE IN INDIA

The nature of Hindu pilgrimage is capsuled in the Indian expression **'Tirthayatra'**, which literally means "undertaking journey to river fords"[2]. Also, a visit to sacred places is considered 'tirthayatra' (Tirtha – Britannica). According to Hindu tradition, a visit to a holy place is not only a physical act but it also implies mental and moral discipline. Pilgrimage to sacred places is accepted as a desirable practice to earn religious merit (phala) within a life lived according to 'dharma'. It is one of the ways towards self-realisation and bliss.

Pilgrimage to a sacred place is of no avail if a person does not lead a moral life. There are many references in Hindu religious literature that suggest moral life as a precondition for deriving any benefit sojourn to holy sanctuaries and bathing in sacred rivers.[3] A journey to sacred places provides opportunity for the householder to detach himself for sometime from the caressed worries of daily life and to devote that time to prayer, contemplation, and listening to the discourses of holy men.

Several views have been expressed by the scholars on the subject of origin and development of the practice of pilgrimage (Tirthayatra). The earliest description of the practice of Hindu pilgrimage (Tirthayatra) in Indian literature is found in the 'Aitareya Brahmana' of the Rig Veda.[4] The Aryan people of the Vedic times revered the rivers, as is clear from the famous river-hymn (nadi stuti) of the Rig Veda.[5] Perhaps, from the Aryan reverence of the rivers grew the concept of 'tirtha' (ford).[6] Bharati believes that pilgrimage proper is not mentioned in the Vedic literature.[7] The practice of 'tirtha yatra' pilgrimage has also been described in the classic Aryan lawbook 'Manusmriti'.

After the Vedic period, the practice of pilgrimage seems to have gained increasing popularity as shown by the great epic Mahabharat (Ca. 300 BC). The Mahabharata clearly considers going on pilgrimages (tirthayatra) superior to sacrifice.

The practice of pilgrimage, with its ancient and diverse origins, continues to be popular among the Hindus. More people are increasingly visiting more sacred places than ever before in the history of India. It is not that the Hindus have become more religious; rather it is because modern means of transportation have made it possible for large number of individuals to undertake pilgrimages. The numbers of pilgrims each year visiting the tirthas is to be reckoned in several crores. Specific occasions, such as the Kumbha Mela, may attract over one crore devout on a particular day.

MOTIVES FOR PILGRIMAGE

The purposes and motives for pilgrimage are so many. These may broadly be classified into two categories. First, there are specific motives concerned with mundane existence. They involve a commitment or vow to the deity (Sukhna) whose blessing is sought for the solution of a problem. 'Mundana' and 'Shradha' also fall under this category.

The second category of motives consists of earning religious merit. It may include holy bath on a specific occasion (Snana), the 'darshan' (sight of the diety), or visiting holy men for spiritual guidance. In the first category of motives, the deity is the focus of pilgrimage, in second, the event of pilgrimage is more significant.

LITERATURE ON PILGRIMAGE PLACES

A lot of literature is available relating to Hindu pilgrimage places in particular. A brief description of the literature is given here. The Mahabharata is the oldest and the most important source of information about the places of pilgrimage in the ancient period. From the description of the tirthas in the Mahabharata, the following conclusions are made:

1. Association of tirthas with water is clearly brought out; most of the sacred spots lie either on river banks, at confluences, or on the sea coast.

2. The tirthas and sacred rivers were spread throughout the country and dedicated people used to visit these holy places.

3. The places of Hindu pilgrimage existed in the areas effectively occupied by people practicing Hindu beliefs.

4. There were clusters of sacred places and the largest number of tirthas were situated in the Ganga basin.

The account of tirthas given in tirthayatra (pilgrimage) section of the epic Mahabharata suggests a grand tour, which includes India and some parts of Pakistan and Afghanistan.

PLACES OF PILGRIMAGE ACCORDING TO THE PURANAS

Next to the epic Mahabharata, the most important sources of information on places of pilgrimage in India, are the Puranas. The Puranas, as a body of Hindu literature, not only possess great sanctity but also contain much more material for the study of culture, history, geography, etc. They provide us great insight into all aspects and phases of Hinduism. Most of the Puranas include in their text important information about the sacred places, rivers, mountains and cities.

The Garuda Purana gives two separate lists of holy places or tirthas. It mentions, in all, eighty one tirthas throughout India out of which sixteen are considered most important tirthas of India. Some tirthas such as Kanyakumari are not mentioned in Garuda Purana. The Matasya Purana gives a comprehensive list of tirthas falling in the region of Narmada.[11]

The Agni Purana also contains a list of sixty two sacred tirthas[12]. Most of the sacred places given in the Agni Purana are situated in northern India and a few in south India.

Places of Pilgrimage in the Medieval Literature

The nine volume digest entitled Krtyakalpataru of Bhatta Lakshmidhara compiled during 1110 A.D. Lists a large number of tirthas spread over the entire country.

Three non-Hindu sources, viz. (1) The Accounts of Hiuan Tsang's travels in India between AD 629 and 645, (2) Alberuni's Kitab-ul-Hind, written in about AD 1030, and (3) Abul Fazal's 'Ain-i-Akbari' of the late sixteenth century give important and reliable information about sacred Hindu places. The seventh century account of Hiuan Tsang provides, among other things, one of the earliest foreign accounts of the institutions and places of pilgrimage in India. From the travels of Hiuan Tsang, it is quite evident that Hindu places of pilgrimage were spread over the entire length and breadth of the country. The Buddhist traveller observed the state of affairs of Hinduism and particularly the sacred places of the Hindus. He noticed the practice of bathing in the sacred rivers, particularly in the Ganga river.

Alberuni in the third decade of the eleventh century AD noticed the institution of pilgrimage and the significance of ritual bathing in Hinduism. Since he remained in the northern part of the country, he mentions the more important sacred places of northern India only.

An important list of major Hindu places of pilgrimage is supplied by Abul Fazal in his celebrated digest on administration entitled 'Ain-i-Akbari' written in the last quarter of the sixteenth century. Abul Fazal gives a concise view of the basic philosophy of the institution of Hindu pilgrimages and attempts to classify and enumerate the more important of these places, particularly in reference to northern India.

IMPORTANT PLACES OF PILGRIMAGE IN INDIA

The institution of pilgrimage to holy places (tirthayatra) is an ancient and continuing religious tradition of the Hindus. Numerous sacred places spread across in various parts of India attract a large number of pilgrims; while some places draw pilgrims from all over the country, others largely from the neighbouring villages. Thus, religion assumes an important role in generating a circulation mechanism in which the entire social strata of Hinduism participates. Religion provides the basis of pilgrimage by offering the reward of unification of the soul and the attainment of objects related to the problems of mundane existence.

Thousands of holy places are scattered throughout India. Some places have more spiritual significance than others. There are four 'Dhamas' or Kingdoms of God, which are Badrinath in North, Rameshwaram in south, Puri in East and Dwarka in west.

There are seven sacred cities known as the 'Saptapuris' (Mokshapuris). The sacred cities are Mathura, Ayodhya, Mayapuri (Haridwar), Kashi (Varanasi), Kanchi (Kanchipuram), Avantipuri (Ujjain and Nasik). The seven most sacred rivers are Ganga, Yamuna, Godavari, Saraswati, Narmada, Sindhu and Kaveri. The eight self-manifested holy places (Swayam Vyakta Khshetras) are Sri Rangam, Triumala, Sri Mushnam and Thotadri in South India; and Shalagram, Pushkara, Naimisaranya and Badrinath in North India.

A discussion on these as well as some other important places follows. Pilgrimage continues to be popular among the Hindus, with its ancient and diverse origins. It may be pointed out that a Hindu has an innate desire to visit at least a few of the hundreds of holy rivers, holy cities, temples and caves as mentioned in their holy scriptures. The number of tirthas in India is so large that the whole of the country can be regarded as a vast sacred space organised into a system of pilgrimage centres.

Modern means of transportation have made it possible for large number of individuals to undertake pilgrimages. The number of pilgrims each year visiting the well-known tirthas is reckoned to be in several crores. Specific occasions, such as Kumbha Mela at Haridwar and Allahabad may attract over one crore devotee's eager to bathe in the sacred rivers.

THE FOUR DHAMAS

There are four Dhamas or abodes/kingdoms of God, which represent Brahmajoti and the Vaikunthas. These are:

(1)   Badrinath

(2)   Puri

(3) Rameshwaram

(4) Dwarka

Badrinath (Badri Ka Ashram) in North

Badrinath is the abode of the Nara and Narayana Rishis. It is situated in the Himalayas on the back of Alakananda, a headstream of the Ganga river. Badrinath is visited by lacs of pilgrims every year in summer. It lies at an elevation of about 10,000 feet. Badrinath is the site of a temple that contains a shrine of Badrinath or Vishnu and has been a well-known pilgrimage centre for more than 2,000 years. Adi Shankaracharya established the fourth and last matth at Joshimatth near Badrinath. The present temple was reinstalled by Adi Shankracharya in the 8th century AD, 1,225 years ago.

Uddhava was sent to Badri Ka Ashram by Lord Krishna.[15] The great rishis Narada, Gautama, Kapila and Kashyapa are said to have come here. Rishis Nara and Narayan performed penances at Badrinath. Sri Ramanujacharya visited Badrinath 955 years ago, Sir Madhvacharya 735 years ago and Sri Nityananda visited Badrinath 500 years ago. During summer about 3,000 pilgrims visit Badrinath per day. Thus, about 2,50,000 pilgrims are visiting this dham every summer season.

Puri (East)

One of the four holy Dhamas, Puri pilgrimage is one of the most essential. The Jagannath temple here is one of the major temples in India. The worship of Lord Jagannath is very ancient. Also known as Sree Purshottam Dham, Sri Kshetra, Puroshottam Kshetra, Nilachal Dham, Jagannath Dham, and Martya Vailkuntha, Puri is located 55 km from Bhubaneshwar in Orissa on the coast of the Bay of Bengal. Sri Ramanujacharya visited Puri between 1107 and 1117 AD, Vishnuswami visited Puri in the second half of twelfth century and established a matth near Markandeshwar tank, known as Vishnuswami matth. Sree

Nimbarkacharya also visited Puri, as also Guru Nanak Dev and many great Acharyas. Shri Chaitanya Mahaprabhu spent 18 years in Puri.

Puri is also a popular tourist resort with very pleasant atmosphere and breathing beaches. The world famous Rath Yatra (Cart festival) attracts about a million pilgrims to Puri. In addition, many other festivals like Chandan Yatra, Snan Yatra, Anavasara festival, etc. attract thousands of pilgrims throughout the year. Every day 56 varieties of 'Bhog' are offered to Lord Jagannath, cooked in the world's largest kitchen in a traditional style. The main temple structure is 214 feet high and is built on elevated ground. The temple complex comprises an area of 10.7 acres and is enclosed by two rectangular walls. There is a wheel on top of the temple made of astadhatu – eight different metals. It is known as the Nilchakra (blue wheel). It is eleven feet an alloy with a circumference of about 36 feet. A flag is mounted every day on a mast attached to the Nilchakra. The main temple is surrounded by 30 different smaller temples. There are four gates – the eastern is known as Singhadwar. The main deities in the temple are of Lord Jagannath, Baldev and Subhadra. Some of the other temples within this temple have the deities of Sri Satya Narayana, Sri Chaitanya, Sri Ramachandra, Sri Gopal, Sri Hanuman, Sri Nrisingha and others.

Rameshwaram (South)

In the south, we have one of the four Dhamas at the south-eastern end of the Indian peninsula. Rameshwaram is on an island, which is in the shape of a conchshell, in the Gulf of Manner. There is a major Lord Shiva temple here called the Ramanathswami temple. The name indicates that Lord Rama visited this place, in Tretayuga. The temple covers an area of 15 acres. The eastern 'gopuram' is 160 feet high. Among the important festivals celebrated here are Mahashivaratri, Brahmotsavam and Thirukalyanam. There is a 3,700 feet long beautiful corridor, which goes around the temple with large sculptured pillars that are elaborately carved. It is the longest temple corridor in India. The corridor is 27 feet high and 17 to 21 feet wide. There is a huge Nandi, the bull carrier of Lord Shiva, in the east. There are 22 teerthams, holy tanks in the temple known by different names. The tradition has been to take a holy dip in all 22 teerthams before going to the Ramananthaswami shrine. There are many temples and shrinas connected with Ramayana in and around Rameshwaram, like Gandhamadana Parvatham, Kothandarma-Swami temple, Dhanushkodi, Darbha Sayanam, Adi Jagannath temple, Lakshmana teertham, Rama teertham.

Dwarka (West): A 'Dham's as well as one of the 'Saptapuris'

In the west, one of the four Dhamas is Dwarka which is also one of the seven holy cities or 'Saptapuris'. Archaeological excavations indicate that Dwarka is built on four former cities. Much of the present town had been submerged by the rising sea levels. There is evidence to suggest that this city was a large port at least as far back as the 15th century B C.

One of the four originals matths founded by Adi Shankaracharya is in Dwarka. Both Shri Ramanujacharya and Shri Madhavacharya visited this place. In the middle of the town is Dwarkadheesh temple. The five storeyed temple is built on 72 pillars. The temple spire is 235 feet high. From the temple dome waves a multicoloured flag decorated with the symbols of the sun and the moon and is 84 feet long. Lord Krishna's great grandson Vajranabha is said to have built the original temple of Dwarkadheesh over Lord Krishna's residential palace. The sanctum of the temple dates back to at least 2,500 years. There are two entrances to the temple. The main entrance is called Mokshadwara. The south entrance is called Swargadwara. Outside this doorway are 56 steps that lead to the Gomati river. The main deity in this temple is of Lord Dwarkadheesh on the central altar. To the right of the main deity presides a big deity of

Pradyaumana and a small deity of Aniruddha, the son and grandson of Lord Krishna. Across Lord Dwarkadheesh temple is a shrine bearing the deity of Devaki, the mother of Lord Krishna. In the back of the main temple on the eastern part of the temple compound are the shrines of Radhika ji, Jamavanti, Satyabhama and Rukmini.

SAPTAPURIS: The Seven Cities

The seven sacred cities or the Saptapuris are the most sacred/ holy cities according to holy scriptures. These are: Ayodhya, Mathura, Haridwar, Kashi, Kanchi, Ujjain and Dwarka.

Ayodhya

It is a very holy city and is an important pilgrimage site. Lord Rama was born and spent much of his time here. At one time, it is said to have had a perimeter of 96 miles and was the capital of Koshala. It is located on the banks of the Saryu river. Ayodhya is 6 km from the town of Faizabad. Rama Janma Bhoomi, where Lord Rama is said to have taken birth, is here. There is a small Lord Rama temple here. There are over 100 temples in Ayodhya.

Janma-sthana is where Lord Rama is said to have been brought up. There is a popular temple dedicated to Hanuman called Hanuman-gadhi. Kanak Bhavan and Kala Rama temple, both have dieties of Sita Rama. There is lush green area by the river surrounding Laksman Ghat. Vashishtha Kund is a temple with a small round kund, like a well. It is at Treth Ka Mandir that Lord Rama is said to have performed yajna. Other temples at Ayodhya are Kshireswara Nath temple and Bharata Kund.

Mathura

Mathura is an extremely important pilgrimage city where Lord Krishna was born. It is 150 km south of Delhi and 14 km from Vrindavan. The main temple here is called the Keshava Deo temple. Vishramaghat is a bathing ghat on the bank of the Yamuna where Krishna rested after killing King Kansa. There is another place called Rangabhumi, where Krishna killed Kansa on the hill called Kansatila. Many pastimes from the Srimad Bhagavatam and other Puranas took place in Mathura.

Haridwar: One of the Saptapuris as well as four places of Kumbha Mela

Haridwar is on the west bank of the Ganga at the foot of the Himalayan mountains. Haridwar means the gateway to Hari (Lord Vishnu). It is also called Ganga-dwara, because the holy Ganga enters the plains here. It is also called Mayapuri Kshetra in the Puranas. It is one of the four places where Kumbha mela is held every 12 years. The places famous in Haridwar are Har Ki Pauri (Brahma Kund), Mansa Devi temple, Bhimgoda kund, Kushavarta ghat, Gaurikund, Kankhal, Daksha Mandir, etc. Hardwar is one of the seven holy cities in India. It is an important pilgrimage town because of its propitious location. Thousands of people come to bathe at Brahm kund on different auspicious occasions.

Kashi (Varanasi)

Varanasi is said to be the oldest inhabited city in the world. There are supposed to be 2000 temples here. It is on the bank of the Ganges, 125 km east of Allahabad. The city was originally called Kashi or the city of lights. It is said that the first jyotirlinga, the fiery pillar of light, came through the earth here and flew into the sky. Therefore, Varanasi is also called Kashi, city of light. The Muslim rulers gave it the name Benares. It is believed that anyone who dies in Varanasi attains moksha (liberation). Many saints and sages have come to Varanasi including Sri Chaitanya Mahaprabhu, Lord Budddha, Sankaracharya and Sri Ramanuja. One of the highlights of a trip here is to see the city from the Ganges waters at sunrise. There is a five-mile parikrama path that goes around this sacred city. There are 81 bathing ghats and other holy kunds or sacred tanks. The important ghats here are

Manikarnika, Dashashwamedha, Panchaganga, Asi Sanga, and Varana Sangam, the most important being Manikarnika, Dashashwamedha and Panchaganga. To bathe there ghats are called Tri-Tirth. Adi Keshava Vishnu temple is located where the Ganga meets the Varana river. Famous temples are Vishvanath temple, Bindhu Madhava, Adi Keshava temple Durga temple and Sankat Mochan temple. The present name of Kashi is Varanasi which is the most important pilgrimage sites in India and also a major tourist attraction.

Its mention is found in the Mahabharata, Ramayana, Srimad Bhagavatam and the Puranas which date back to 5,000 years.

Varanasi is a centre of learning especially for Sanskrit scholars. Sarnath is 10 km away and is famous for the place where Lord Buddha first preached about enlightenment twenty five centuries ago. The famous Shiva temple is called Vishwanath Temple (Golden Temple) and is visited by a large number of pilgrims.

Kanchi (Kanchipuram)

Kanchipuram is known as the 'Golden City of Temples'. It is considered one of the seven main sacred cities of India. It has over a hundred temples and is believed to give eternal happiness to one who goes there. It is said that 'Ka' (Brahma) 'Anchi' (worshipped) Lord Vishnu at this place and that is why the city was given the name Kanchi while Puram means 'city'. Kanchi was the capital of the Pallavas from 7th to 9th centuries. The city is divided into two main parts Sivakanchi and Vishnukanchi. Kailasanath and Vaikuntha Perumal temples were the most important temples built by the Pallavas, Varadaraja. Kamakshi and Ekambareswara temples were originally built by the Cholas but were added onto by the Vijayanagar and Nayak rulers. There are thirteen Divya Desam temples in the area of Kanchipuram, namely Sri Vaikuntha Perumal temple, Sri Varadaraja Swami temple, Sri Adi Varaha Perumal temple, Sri Deeparakast temple,

Sri Vathoktakari temple Sri Alagiyasingar temple, Sri Nilathingal Thundalthan Peruma temple and others. Kanchipuram is also known as Satyavrata Kserta due to Aswamedha sacrifice performed here by Lord Brahma. Throughout its history, Kanchipuram also remained one important pilgrimage centre[25].

Ujjain: One of the Saptapuris, a place of Kumbha Mela and a Jyotirlinga

Ujjain is situated on the bank of the Shipra river, which is one of the westernmost tributaries of Ganga. It is said that Lord Shiva killed the demon Tripura at Ujjain. Ujjain is the place where Sandipani Muni instructed Lord Krishna and Balarama. It was called Avantipuri when Lord Krishna studied here. Gopal Mandir is a famous Krishna temple with a silver deity. This temple was constructed by Maharaja Adul Rao Scindia's queen in the 19th century. The Kumbh Mela in Ujjain is held in Chaitra (March-April). About 3 million people come here for bathing.[15]

Mahabaleswar temple of Ujjain is famous which contains one of the 12 Shiva Jyotirlingas. It attracts thousand of pilgrims and is by far the most visited temple in Ujjain.

Twelve Jyotirlingas

There are 12 Jyotirlingas spread in different parts of India, which are mentioned in Shiv Puran, Ramayan, Mahabharata and Skandha Puran.[16] They appeared as the sacred places and are the symbols of creation and are innumerable, but twelve of these are very important.

According to Puranas, following twelve Jyotirlingas[17] bear great religious merit (Mahayatmya).

1. Shri Som Nath in Sourashtra, Gujarat

2. Shri Mallikarjun in Kurnool district, Andhra Pradesh.

3. Shri Mahakaleshwar in Ujjain (M.P.)

4. Shri Omkareshwar in Malwa (M.P.)

5. Shri Kedar Nath in the Himalayas (U.P.)

6. Shri Vishweshwar (Vishwanath) in Varanasi (U.P.)

7. Shri Trimbakeshwar, near Nasik in Maharashtra

8. Shri Baidyanath in Bihar

9. Shri Nageshwar in Gujarat

10. Shri Rameshwar in Tamil Nadu

11. Shri Ghrishneshwar in Swalaya near Ellora Caves, Maharashtra

12. Shri Lingaraj in Bhubneshwar.

Fifty One Shakti Peethas

Puranas describe Shakti Peethas as places where the ornaments and parts of body of Sati, consort of Lord Shiva, fell. Those places became divine and places of pilgrimage. These places are scattered all over the Indian subcontinent. Following is the list[18] of Shakti Peethas:

1. Bhairvi Shakti Peeth at Hingulas near Baluchistan

2. Bimla Devi at Vat Nagar in West Bengal

3. Uma Shakti Devi at Bhuteshwar (Mathura)

4. Mahisha in Kolhapur (Maharashtra)

5. Sunanda Devi in Bangladesh

6. Aparna Devi in Bangladesh

7. Shri Sundri in Ladakh

8.   Vishalakashi in Varanasi

9.   Vishveshi in Andhra Pradesh

10. Gandaki Devi in Nepal

11. Naraini Devi near Kanyakumari

12. Varahi Devi

13. Jwalamukhi in Himachal Pradesh

14. Avanti Devi in Madhya Pradesh

15. Phullara Devi in West Bengal

16. Bhramri Bhadrakali in Nasik (Maharashtra)

17. Mahamaya Devi in Amarnath Cave (Kashmir)

18. Nandini Devi near Burdhman (West Bengal)

19. Mahalakshmi at Mahklarjun (Andhra Pradesh)

20. Mahakali (Kalika) on Howrah line at Nalhati station

21. Uma Mahadevi Midhileshiwari in Midhila

22. Kumari in Tamil Nadu

23. Chander-Bhaga Devi at Girnar

24. Tripur-Malini Devi at Jallandhar (Punjab)

25. Shivani at Chittrakut

26. Jai Durga at Vaidyanth (Bihar)

27. Mahishmardini near Burdhman

28. Devi Sharvani at Kanyakumari

29. Bahula Devi in West Bengal

30. Bhawani in Bangladesh

31. Devi Mangal-Chandi at Ujjain

32. Gayati Devi at Pushkar (Rajasthan)

33. Dakashayani Manas- Peeth at Mansarovar

34. Yasho-reshwari in Bangladesh

35. Lalita Devi at Allahabad (Paryag)

36. Vimla in Jagannath Temple, Puri

37. Dev-Garbha Kali at Shivkanchi, Kanchipuram

38. Kali – Place unknown

39. Devi Narmada at Amar Kantak

40. Kamakhya at Guwahati

41. Mahamaya Guhyeshvari in Nepal

42. Jayanti Devi near Shillong

43. Sarvanandakari Patneshwari at Patna

44. Bhramari Devi near Jalpaiguri (West Bengal)

45. Tripur Sundri in Tripura

46. Kapalini near Midnapur (West Bengal)

47. Savitri in Kurukshetra

48. Indrekhi in Sri-Lanka

49. Bhoot Dhatri near Burdwan

50. Ambika, 70 km from Jaipur

51. Kalika Devi in Calcutta

Hem Kund Sahib one of the most reversed of all sikh shrines where Guru Gobind Singh performed meditation.

REFERENCES

1. Bhardwaj, S.M., 'Hindu Places of Pilgrimage in India', Surjeet Publication, Delhi (1989), p.2.

2. Quoted in Poddar, H.P. (Ed.), 'Kalyan Tirthank' Geeta Press, Gorakhpur (1957), p.31.

3. The Brahmanas are "expiratory Liturgical texts" attached to the Vedas. The period of composition of the Rigveda is usually considered to be between 1500 and 1000 BC.

4. Rig Veda, 75.5, as quoted in 'Kalyan Tirthank' op. cit., p.4.

5. Bhardwaj, S.M. op. cit., p.4.

6. Agehananda Bharti, Pilgrimage in the India Tradition, University of Washington Press (1963), p. 137.

7. The Mahabharata expressly says:

    O thou best of Bharta race, sojourns in tirthas which are meritorious. And which contribute one of the high mysteries of Rishis are even superior to the sacrifice. Roy, P.C. The Mahabharata, Vol. II, 175.

8. Bhardwaj, S.M. op. cit., pp. 32 – 33.

9. Winternitz M.A. History of Indian Literature, p. 529.

10. Garuda Purana, Chaps. 66 and 81.

11. Dikshitar Purana The Matsya Purana – A Study, p. 24.

12. Agni Purana (in Sanskrit), edited by Rajendralala Mitra, Vol. III.

13. Aiyangar, K.V.R., ed. Katyakalpatorn, Tirthavivecana Kandam, Introduction, pp. XIX. Ff.

14. See Encyclopaedia Britannica, 1998.

15. See India – A Travel Survival Kit (4th edition), Lonely Planet Publications, Australlia (1990).

16. Quoted in, Poddar, H.P., (ed.) Kalyan Tirthank, op. cit., p. 463.

17. Ibid, page 463.

18. Ibid, p. 516.

19. India – A Travel Survival Kit (4 Ked.), op. cit., p. 774.

20. The Information supplied by the Directorate of Tourism, J&K Government.

21. According to Hindu holy books there are three most sacred places of pilgrimage (tirthas) called 'Tirsthli'. These are Prayag, Kashiand Haridwar.

22. Kumbh Mela is like a "Yogi convention", where Yogis, Sadhus, holy people and pilgrims come from various places.

23. Sherring , M.A., *'Benares – The sacred city of the Hindus'*, Low Price Publications, Delhi (1990), p. 139.

24. John Howley, *'Holy Places and Temples in India'*, John Howley and Spiritual Guide USA (1998), p. 412.

25. Encyclopedia Britannica CD (1994 + 1998).

CHAPTER
16

HIMALAYAS AND ADVENTURE TOURISM

JOGINDER SINGH[*]

Mountains are one of the vital mainstays of life on our planet earth. Approximately, 10% of the world population lives in the mountain regions but more than 40% is dependent in some way upon mountain resources including water, mineral wealth, forestry, agriculture and recreation. The actual number of people living within mountain regions is difficult to verify. This is in part because large-scale migration is taking place continuously in many highland areas. The more important fact is that almost half the world's population, whether living within or adjacent to mountainous areas, depends upon mountain resources or is influenced by processes going on within the mountains.

Mountains have fascinated me and attracted me from my childhood. I was born in Sialkot, which was then in pre-partition days, the gateway for going to Kashmir via Jammu. From our house

---

[*] Member - Himalayan Tourism Advisory Board (HIMTAB), Govt. of India.

we could see the mountains in the distance – beckoning and inviting. Every year during summers our family used to move to some hill station – Kashmir, Dalhouise, Dharamsala, etc.

HIMALAYAS

The Himalayas are the youngest mountains on earth and, therefore, the highest. They have not yet gone through the process of erosion like other mountains. On the contrary they are still rising. Sixty million years ago a plate of earth's crust carrying the Indian landmass travelled 5000 kms from near the South Pole and collided with Laurasia. The two continental landmasses pushed the colliding surface upwards – resulting in the most gigantic upheaval – the forming of the Himalayas. The most substantial rise took place in the past 38 million years and the final uplift has occurred in the past one million years.

To describe the grandeur of the Himalayas, I quote "Himalayas demand the superlatives". They are superlatives, the highest mountain, the highest pass, the deepest gorge, the highest living animals – these mountains confront us with phenomena that exist nowhere else on earth. Other mountains can be digested by landscape. They are penetrable, harnessed by roads and railways. But no railways cross the Himalayas and only a few roads have been able to penetrate. These mountains are so stupendous that they can be over crossed, but not tunnelled, climbed but never tamed, mapped but seldom visited.

Kenneth Mason in his famous book "Abode of Snow" has called them "the greatest physical feature of the earth".

The titanic forces that formed the Himalayas also created an extraordinary complex environment exercising a very powerful influence upon the entire subcontinent. The health and fertility of the entire region is totally dependent upon the natural conditions in the Himalayas, which protect the Indian subcontinent from the harsh cold Siberian winds blowing from the north, and the eternal snowmelt feeds the rivers which are the very life-line of the region. They are undoubtedly the main guardians and donors of the rainfall and water supply in this area. They also produce their own climate ranging from near polar in the higher reaches to a tropical humid one in the foothills. The winter snows are stored for feeding the perennial rivers. The climatic and geologic variety has contributed towards creation of diverse ecosystems ranging from the cold desert of Ladakh to the tropical rainforests of Arunachal Pradesh and comprising an enormous wealth of natural living and non-living resources.

Ideal Holiday Destination

After all what is a holiday? It is a change from your immediate surrounding and environment. People ask me why an adventure holiday? I tell them that when you are engaged in a sport of adventure your full and complete attention is focussed on what you are presently doing. If you are climbing a mountain all your mind is alive to finding and looking for footholds and handholds which could take you up; if you are trekking you are all concerned about reaching your destination. In short, such activity affords you a complete and total break from your immediate past. It takes you away from all your cares and worries and when you return, you come back as a new person refreshed, relaxed and recharged, ready to face challenges and stress and strain of the modern day life anew. Himalayas have everything, which a discerning tourist could look for – from the most leisurely to the most adventurous and challenging tours.

Let us first define what the Himalayas Tourism is all about. Obviously, it means tourist traffic both domestic as well as international to the Himalayas. Such tourists could be trekkers, mountaineers, photographers, botanists, zoologists, writers, artists, poets and even scientists. It also includes those who visit Himalayan towns and stay enjoying the grandeur and scenic beauty of the mountains.

I would, however, confine my talk to the adventure segment of the Himalayan Tourism. What is so fascinating about the Himalayas? How is it that people from all walks of life are drawn to the Himalayas? Different people have different answers to this. I cannot do better than to quote Lionel Terray, a great French mountaineer, who said *"I hurried still more not to miss the vision for which we had come so far. Then the morale happened. Folded in light mist, hill after hill rolled away into the distance from beneath my feet and over this green ocean sparkled the vast icebergs of the Himalayas. Never in my remotest dreams had I imagined such beauty could exist on earth.. ... time effaces all memories, but the feelings of that moment are branded in me while I live.... Looking back today I see more that it was not only the revelation of my dreams of youth but the beginning of an experience which has influenced me more than almost any other... the discovery of... a world outside our time"*.

There are a number of sports and activities that one could indulge in while in the mountains.

Mountaineering

Himalayas are the mecca for the mountaineers, world over. It has not only some of the highest peaks like Everest, K2 but some of the most beautiful ones also like Kanchenjunga, Nanda Devi, Neelkantha. The famous mountain climber Willi Unsoeld was so fascinated by the beauty of Nanda Devi that he named his daughter after it. Mountaineers will come to the Himalayas year after year in quest of their own climbing ambitions. Unfortunately, mountaineering gear and equipment of international standard is not produced in India as yet. The expeditions have to bring their own equipment with them and carry it back. Secondly, reliable and adequate maps of the Himalayan region are not available due to security reasons but the same are freely available in the international market. This anomaly needs to be addressed and resolved.

Trekking

Trekking is a very healthy sport. It affords exercise to the limbs and muscles of the body and at the same time it provides congenial environment and atmosphere for thinking and mental reflection. After all, it is the most natural way of travelling for man. With the passage of time and faster means of transportation coming in, we have become more and more ease loving. The joys and thrills of walking slowly, observing and savouring the countryside have been lost to us. It is only in the mountains and specially the Himalayas where such development has not so far reached and you can still walk and trek in close communion with nature. The hill folks are simple, innocent and disarmingly charming. They still live their life as the Creator intended us to lead... pure, simple and down-to-earth. Mountains are great equalisers; the rich and the poor, the high and the mighty all are cut to size and brought down to a common denominator – trek on the same trails for moving from one place to another. That is the reason why you find camaraderie and willing response for participation in community work, functions and festivals with such gay abandon in the hills.

Biking

Mountain biking has become quite popular with the foreign tourists visiting Himalayas. Unfortunately, they are obliged to bring their own mountain bikes with them because good quality mountain bikes are not available here. There is a tremendous scope even in the domestic market, for popularising this sport. It has the advantage of mobility and speed especially when going downhill, yet it is slow enough to observe and enjoy the scenic beauty, the local culture, customs and traditions around you as you wind your way as you like. And then you can stop when and wherever you like.

Camping

Camping is the most ideal way of having a most satisfying mountain holiday. You can select a site of your own choice affording you ample opportunities in your favourite pastime and hobbies like walking, photography, painting, angling, etc. The biggest advantage is that you are not tied to the same place. You can move to another location any time you wish to do so.

River Rafting

River rafting or white water rafting as it is called in some countries is a new adventure sport which has caught the imagination of the people the world over. It has now become increasingly popular in the Himalayan rivers and especially so in the rivers Indus, Ladakh, Spiti, Beas in Himachal, river Tons in Uttranchal, Teesta in Sikkim, Brahmaputra and of course the most popular rafting site on river Ganga near Rishikesh. It is encouraging to find thousands of Indian adventurers participating in this sport for the thrill of it. Many corporate offices now send their executives for such adventure holidays to infuse in them a spirit of adventure, initiative as well as self-confidence.

Paragliding

This sport originated as hang-gliding and has now developed into paragliding. The advantage is that the paraglide can be folded and carried in a small handbag, which can be taken to any vantage point for a launch, taking advantage of the upward thermal thrust. This sport is gradually gaining popularity.

Skiing

Skiing has now become popular in the Himalayas for the skiing enthusiasts. The skiing sites are Gulmarg in Kashmir, Auli near Joshimath in Garhwal, Kufri near Shimla, etc. Way back in seventies Mr Santner, the Swiss expert, was invited by the Govt. of India to carry out a survey in the Himalayan regions to find out the best locations for skiing. According to him, Solang Nala near Manali could provide skiing scope throughout the year even during the summer months.

Himalayan Tourism & Himachal

Himachal holds the place of pride in the field of Himalayan Tourism since long because of its fascination by the tourists. Previously all pilgrims to Kailash Mansarover went via Kinnaur over Shipki La route, which was appropriately called Hindustan Tibet Road. Even the British found it most enchanting and set up the maximum number of hill stations here – Kasauli, Dagshai, Salathoo, Shimla, Dalhousie. Shimla especially became synonymous with a holiday since in British time it was India's summer capital when the entire Government used to move to Shimla during summers. Kalka/Shimla narrow gauge rail link was specially laid to facilitate travel between Delhi and Shimla. Now the Kinnaur valley and the Kullu valley are hot favourites with tourists – be it mountaineering, trekking, camping, and skiing, heli-skiing, paragliding or even river rafting.

Himalayan Conservation

The local human communities have evolved rich culture often adapting themselves to hostile environment with remarkable resilience. Such an immense variety of resources are the greatest and also the most vulnerable assets of the Himalayas, because the young mountain chain has a very fragile ecosystem, highly susceptible to any thoughtless intrusion and meddling which would upset this precariously balanced ecosystem. The hill people have adapted themselves to survive in those peculiar conditions where temperature varies from place to place and hour to hour. The air is so clear thus rendering the radiation so intense that you are susceptible to suffering sunstroke in the day and frostbite at night. In Ladakh during summers you can cross streams before noon only because by afternoon they become raging torrents in flood due to the snowmelt in the higher reaches caused by the scorching sun rays at those heights.

Why people want to go to the Himalayas? Because they are beautiful, serene, giving you a strange feeling of being at peace with yourself. The hill people are cheerful, simple and hospitable. It is, therefore, only fair that we should leave the Himalayas as beautiful and as attractive as we found them. Himalayan environmental conservation is a special subject by itself. I would confine myself only to saying to all visitors "This Unique Creation of God, the Himalayas, are your host. Abide by their culture and traditions and leave them as clean and beautiful as you found them".

CHAPTER
17

EXOTIC TOURISM: THE EMERGING PARADIGM

PURNIMA CHAUHAN*

Mass tourism may have catapulted the tourism industry to the number one position as the foremost forex spinner but it looms as a grave threat to the environment and hence to itself. The change being wrought by forces of liberalisation, globalisation and information technology is perceptible in the emergence of a new tourism paradigm globally, which is called 'Exotic tourism'. The growing demand segment of up-market tourists with no budgetary constraints for getting a novelty experience throws up exciting possibilities of developing tourism wherein suppliers will automatically conserve the environment since it has the potential to yield unimaginable profits by value adding innovatively. Their inherent exclusivity makes such instances rare but the rapid communication network may actually help crystallise this trend very soon. To derive maximum mileage from this phenomenon

* Former Secretary, State Election Commission, Himachal Pradesh.

the State will have to be proactive in its tourism strategies and policies.

Tourism is emerging as the largest global industry in the post-World War economic scenario. It is further slated to gain even more global primacy in the 21st century overtaking the oil and the motor vehicles industries. From a meagre 21 million tourist arrivals in 1950 the number has catapulted to nearly 700 million by 1998. Since tourism has a significant impact in catalysing employment growth, environmental regeneration, development of remote areas, providing women and other disadvantaged groups with a new means of livelihood, besides promoting social integration, it is vital to the growth of any economy especially of developing countries. For developing economies like India that are caught in the throes of disparate cultures, concerns and needs while coping with economic transition wrought by the triple forces of globalisation, liberalisation and technological revolution, tourism growth could have a positive multiplier effect.

According to Jean Claude Baumgarten, president WTTC, "India's travel and tourism industry has the potential to be India's no.1 economic driver." The positive tourism multiplier effect has the capacity to generate 32 million jobs in India. Currently it provides 9.1 million jobs, i.e. 2.4% of the total Indian labour force being the 2nd largest spin-off in the world. The labour capital ratio per million rupees of investment in hotels and restaurants yields 89 jobs as against 44 in agriculture and 12.06 in manufacturing. Nearly 80% of the tourism-generated jobs are of small and medium level. But it is significant to note that each job directly resulting from tourism activity further creates 11 indirect jobs. Moreover, large corpus of entry-level jobs are suitable for women. These job opportunities are geographically spread out thereby balancing the skewed development. These jobs are even likely to survive the onslaught of the technology revolution. Such forecasts and development indicators are ample reason for India to reorient its development strategies to draw maximum mileage form the tourism industry. However, center-staging tourism as a catalyst for spurring economic development could jeopardise its own existence by endangering the very environment from which tourism draws its basic sustenance. Will concerns like environmental impact increase if developing countries are tempted to indiscriminately exploit the tourism product for enchasing quickly on its socio-economic growth potential?

Hence while the galloping growth figures of tourist arrivals and receipts are a welcome trend, it is important to envision the direction that tourism development is likely to take. There has to be a clear policy on whether we want quantity or quality of tourists or a mix of both. Tourism cannot be flogged until it becomes unremunerative or endangers itself. Tourism is essentially an intangible and fragile product normally considered a luxury spin-off from other more brasstacks of socio-economic political activities. Buffeted by dynamic socio-economic political changes ushered in by the globalisation, liberalisation and the technological revolution, modern tourism confronts us with the following questions today:

▶ The moot question is that if mass tourism is a threat to the environment and consequently to tourism itself then how does one check its growth?

▶ Can a new tourism focus alter the tide of environmental degradation which endangers not only the sustainability but the very existence of the tourism product? Perhaps the answer lies in developing what I choose to call exotic tourism.

▶ Do we envision a thrust on exotic/designer/eco-tourism product as a viable option for sustaining the future of tourism?

▶ Are tourism strategies, policies and infrastructure flexible enough to foresee and gear up to meet this challenge?

▶ Would the future tourism product envisage a role shedding by government to the advantage of the private operators for a new and fruitful partnership between these two role players?

Notwithstanding this quest to define the future of the tourism product, the enduring concern which will prevail is that, mass tourism forms the backbone, the very bread and butter of the tourism industry worldwide. Hence it cannot be wished away despite its proven negative impact on the environment. We need to rid ourselves of the mind-set that tourism has only a positive spin-off. Mass tourism is certainly an environmental threat. Moreover, preconceived optimism about tourism revenues ignores the need for interventionist policies and strategies required to anticipate and mitigate its likely negative fallout on the socio-economic and environmental fronts.

Environmental impact assessments of tourism activities are gaining increasing legitimacy today, dispelling the complacency that nature's bounty is an inexhaustible, renewable resource. The costs of such profligacy will be an increasing burden borne by the users unless they focus immediately on reversing environmentally unfriendly practices. Environment conservation efforts alone can guarantee the long-term sustainability of the fragile tourism product. But the rapid strides made by mass tourism today focus only on the swelling profit margins oblivious to the fact that ignoring the negative fallout of upsetting this delicate nature balance will be an act of *hara kiri* for the tourism industry.

Fortunately, mass tourism is a follower, not a natural leader unlike exotic tourism. Hence mass tourism will gradually follow where exotic leads. Therefore, tourism policy and strategy has to be focused on exotic tourism because ingenuity is the basic ingredient needed here to encash on the novelty factor before the exotic destination/ activity loses its charm after being overtaken by mass tourist hoarders.

What is driving exotic tourism today? Globalisation, liberalisation and technological revolution have opened up new vistas even in economy closeted for years behind the Iron and Bamboo curtains. In Maslow's hierarchy, tourism is positioned along with higher drivers like social, esteem, recognition and self-actualisation needs. The very up-market tourist segment occupies the topmost need slot. For him, the novelty factor is an essential motivator, which drives the demand for exclusivity giving birth to exotic or alternative tourism. The supplier's skill lies in breaking away from the beaten track and customising the tourism product around this client's lifestyle to enable realising even his most nebulous dream. With the world getting more homogenised by shrinking to a global village, the novelty factor has become so vital that it has been upscaled to be distinguished as exotic tourism catering to the *crème de la crème* of the society.

It is this class of tourists who fuel tourism growth into hitherto uncharted directions. Since their exotic desires are not bridled by budgetary constraints, financially it is extremely viable for the tourism provider/ supplier to spin every such fancy into reality. This does not come cheap. But the premium placed on exclusivity by such target tourists is so high that there is ample incentive to value-add to such tourism products through extremely innovative customisation.

The most recent example is the American space tourist, Dennis Tito who is the proud solitary member of the most exclusive club of space-tourists! It will be a long wait until another member is inducted to share the limelight. The prohibitive cost, risk and hi-tech training which are essential prerequisites to realising such a dream have put Dennis in an enviable league. The resultant media hype and global recognition that it has generated is perhaps more than adequate pay-off to this elite tourist for the cost and risk he incurred to indulge his whim.

Virtual arenas of yesterday are fast converted into concrete possibilities of today by imaginative interface between tourism infrastructure and internet technology. The new kids on the block with fat cat corporate salaries and fancy perks earned from high stress jobs do not want to tread the beaten track when they want to unwind on a holiday. Their holiday component is as much a status symbol as their new Ferraris. This 'global village' is whetting appetites for Star Trek tourism 'to venture where no man has gone before'.

Providers are going overboard to encash on these phenomena. With a no holds barred budget, fancies take flight and nothing is too bizarre to be created for such a client. Competition in this sector is fierce with the convergence of communication and information technology providing instant access to relatively unknown vistas at the click of a button. It has radically changed the way tourism products are sourced, evaluated, bought and consumed. This too has whetted the wanderlust of the present generation. They are more inclined to experiment with the unknown. Doing something different or doing the same thing differently has become the new credo of survival in this cutthroat, competitive market-place.

From modest sand dune surfing/ skiing to resorts hollowed out in mountains, the provider has become the genie regularly rubbing Alladin's lamp. His whole focus is to promote his jet set image of having arrived since he has 'done it all, seen it all', the capacity to indulge in one's whims imaginatively with the concomitant media blitz gives the target person an incomparable psychological edge well above the *hoi polloi* of society.

Since the investment and its return from such an elitist target group is likely to be very high, the provider too takes pains to preserve and nurture his novel tourism destination/ activity to be able to extract maximum cash mileage from this golden goose. He knows that if and when such a destination/ activity is inevitably discovered, cloned and invaded by hoarders of mass tourism, the value of his product will plummet to zero. The huge profit margins are directly correlated to conserving the natural ambience of the novel tourism product. Hence, the exotic tourism supplier suddenly dons the *avatar* of an avid conservationist.

Obviously heavy investments in this fragile sector will only be forthcoming if the idea supplied has instant appeal as being off the beaten track. Moreover, to ensure recovery of investment, the idea has to be sold quickly to interested affluent clients before it loses its novelty. Take the case of the identical Palm Islands being developed in the shape of palm trees off the coast of Dubai at a whopping cost of US $ 1.5 million for the first phase alone! The islands will be visible to the naked eye even from the moon! The trunk of the islands will incorporate a marine park where dolphins and whales will romp to the delight of the tourist. Nearly 40 boutique hotels on each island with scope for 2000 condominium type homes and villas on each man-made protective reef are planned. Each villa will cost approximately US $ 550,000 and is being offered on long lease already! Significantly the ecosystem of the reef will not be endangered. In fact, being a Unique Selling Proposition of the project it will evolve to provide a sanctuary for sea and bird life.

The supplier's skill lies in providing such novel experiences to his client without saturating his wanderlust, rather whetting it further! The recent emergence of 'event management' services was a tentative step in this direction. Event managers succeeded in tailoring an event around a predetermined theme. Imaginatively packaged reality as a theme for shows staged by companies like 'Wizcraft' proved to be a big draw. Then came the idea of 'virtual reality'. Just by donning special goggles, one undertakes a brief journey into simulated exciting domains of super hero comics and science fiction. Somewhere along this process, the dividing line between fact and fiction is getting blurred. Bizarre ideas like the 'underwater hotels' off the Florida coast and Atlantis in the Bahamas; 'ice hotels' in Canada and Sweden complete with beds made of ice-blocks; the 'salt hotel' in Bolivia; the 'underground hotel' at Broken Hill in Australia; the 'Vedic city' in Iowa; the 'cave dwelling' developed in Turkey... all are inspirations from the realm of fairyland.

Very recently a tourist operator submitted a proposal to obtain government clearances to hire a mountain in a picturesque Himalayan landscape for hosting a non-stop 'Retro-Party' atop the peak! His endeavour is to be the first to implement this idea and enter the Guinneass Book of World Records. His market survey has revealed that there are adequate number of very affluent personalities enthusiastic in endorsing this idea. Their famous persona will immediately attract the paparazzi to cover this once in a lifetime event. Confronted by this novel idea, the government is trying to comprehend the kind of clearances it will have to provide while simultaneously advocating necessary precautions. The publicity advantage and likely revenue accruals are yet to be estimated.

It is evident that the development of this variety of tourism cannot be the exclusive preserve of either the private operator or the State. Both have to work in tandem since the State owns most of these exclusive tourism preserves but lacks the skills inherent in a private sector supplier to create value additions upon these assets and market them in a fashion in confluence with the lifestyle of the targeted very up-market tourist. Hence tourism policy and strategy will have to recognise that it is exotic tourism which will chart the future of tourism.

This idea is likely to take a lot of creative brainstorming to crystallise. The role-playing that is required of the government, especially the bureaucracy, will necessitate rethinking and dispensing with old-fashioned regulatory mechanisms. Simple regulations charting a more transparent and proactive path in the tourism policy and strategy will go a long way in attracting such up-market investments. Flexible policies drawn up in mutually beneficial partnerships between the private and government sector alone will be able to prevent the ongoing exploitation of the planet and reap the windfall harvest likely from such innovative virtual tourism. Recently, there was a welcome shift in the tourism strategy of India from 'one country one policy' to each of India's 28 states identifying their own USPs and aggressively developing and promoting their particular niche markets.

In fact tourism and environment have travelled together parallelly since long. The time has now come for them to blend as 'ecotourism' or 'exotic tourism' which is bold, up-market, exclusive, tailor-made and charts out new unexplored niches to cater to the future tourism needs of the very affluent class. If we do not deploy the concept of 'exotic tourism' to tread gingerly towards this newly forged alliance we will jeopardise both – the future of tourism and its ambient environment; an environment which is fast degenerating under the burden of the criminal indifference of the exploitative, low paying, mass tourism industry.

CHAPTER

18

TOURISM IN JAMMU REGION – PROBLEMS AND PROSPECTS

DESH BANDHU GUPTA*

INTRODUCTION

Jammu region extending from Lakhanpur to Banihal and Poonch to Paddar is a land of myriad interests. A combination of hilly and plain areas, the region varies in its climate, culture and customs from one place to another. Its climate is pleasant at higher mountains as compared to the tropical heat on its outer hills in summer. Winter marches with severe chill in hilly areas but a touch of warmth is still there in the plains. It is propagated that the region has numerous ideal places for picnics and quiet holidays unfurling their own unique breathtaking beauty that hypnotises the visitors. Interested parties in tourism industry project the

* Professor in Commerce, Incharge PG Degree in Tourism Department of Management Studies, University of Jammu.

tourism product or the region in the shape of places of pilgrimage, scenic splendour, charming culture, hospitality, history, art and unexplored and untouched places.

Objectives of the Study

1. To study the tourism product of the region.

2. To study the problems and prospects of the tourism industry in the region.

3. To suggest tools and techniques for the development of tourism industry in the region smoothly.

Scope of the Study

The present paper is a micro case study of tourism industry in Jammu region only. An elementary attempt has been made to understand the tourism product of the region from host's and visitor's point of view analytically. Future prospects of the industry, problems in the development of the industry and the tools and techniques for the smooth growth of the industry in the region are few other aspects of the study.

Limitations of the Study

1. The paper may have a greater element of subjectivity of the author which can be a subject of major criticism.

2. Many areas of importance may remained untouched.

3. Few of the observations are based upon old survey conducted by the author.

4. Time is a major limiting factor.

5. The paper is based mostly on secondary data and observations.

6. Primary and secondary data in certain cases is not available.

NATURE OF THE TOURISM INDUSTRY IN THE REGION

1. Jammu region, the Gateway to Kashmir valley, attracts lakhs of pilgrims from every nook and corner of the country to famous 'Shri Mata Vaishno Devi Shrine'.

2. Before the onset of terror in the State by the militants, lakhs of domestic tourists used to pass Jammu region enroute to Kashmir valley.

3. All tourists visiting Jammu and Kashmir state by rail or road have to pass Jammu region before entering other parts of the state.

4. Majority of the tourists in Jammu region are pilgrims.

5. Shri Mata Vaishno Devi Shrine is the most preferred destination for lakhs of pilgrims in the region every year.

6. In recent times, pilgrim traffic to Shri Mata Vaishno Devi Shrine is changing its character from seasonal to annual phenomenon due to the improved en route facilities from Katra (the base camp) to the cave.

7. Most preferred time for pilgrimage to Shri Mata Vaishno Devi cave is 'Navratras' falling in the March and September/ October.

8. An important event of the region, viz. annual fare at Jhiri on Kartik Purnima lacks proper statistics and publicity.

9. Most of the places of the region are unknown to the outside world.

10. Infrastructural facilities at the potential tourist resorts are not adequately provided/ developed.

11. Picnics and excursions are the activities mostly undertaken by the local population.

12. Tourists in the region can be classified into four categories:

    i)   Local tourists/ pilgrims belonging to the region.

    ii) Tourists/ pilgrims from the other regions of the state.

    iii) Tourists/ pilgrims from the other parts of India.

    iv) International/ foreign tourists/ pilgrims.

13. Lakhs of local tourists/pilgrims visit different pilgrimage places like Shahadra Shrief, 'Shiv Khori', Aghar Jitto, Budda Amar Nath, Kaplas Kund, Machail Yatra, Pingla Devi, Baba Farid-ud-din and his son Isser-ud-din (Urs-Shah), Sudh Maha Devi, etc., within the region every year.

14. Revenue generated through pilgrimage/ tourism in the region has very low multiplier effect as it seeps away quickly to the other parts of the state/country.

15. Very few items of the region are popular as souvenir among pilgrims/tourists.

16. Tourism has been recognised as an industry for some purposes in the region. It has its own direct and indirect effects which are still poorly understood and even less well controlled.

17. Most of the region is hilly and has difficult access.

18. Many places offering quietude tourism in the region are unexplored.

19. Outside tourists are not clear about the geographical position of the region.

20. Terrorism is active at certain places in the region offering excellent tourist resorts.

21. Climate of Jammu district and part of Kathua district is quite hot in summer.

22. The region has not identified itself with anything except Vaishno Devi cave and to some extent with 'Bhadarwahi' Rajmash.

23. Food offered to the tourists in the region is Punjabi and not of the region, viz. Dogri.

24. The region at present has very few new things to offer to the pilgrims/tourists.

25. Efforts for the promotion of tourism in the region by the Government agencies and the private agencies need coordination.

26. Long-term policy for the development of tourism in the region is missing.

27. People of the region in general are not clear about their role in tourism development and tourism product of the region.

28. Percentage of pilgrim-cum-tourism is very small in the total pilgrimage traffic to the Vishnu Devi shrine.

29. At the first instant, people of the region resist any change.

30. Cheating, overcharging, corruption, misbehaviour is overtaking the professionalism in tourism industry.

Some Facts About the Region

1. Tourist resorts of the region are alternatives and not the substitutes of Kashmir valley's resorts.

2. Carrying capacity of all resorts in the region is very less as compared to that of Kashmir valley.

3. Region lacks good/big lakes like Dal and Wular or the Kashmir valley.

4. Historically too, region finds second place in comparison to Kashmir valley.

5. Region faces a stiff competition from the state of Himachal Pradesh.

6. Rich Dogra culture has been invaded by mixed modern culture in the towns.

7. Region is under threat from militants.

8. Before the hold of militancy in the Valley, the region was not in the priority list of Government agenda for tourism development.

9. Overtaking of Shri Mata Vaishno Devi cave by the Shri Mata Vaishno Devi Shrine Board under dynamic leadership, the Gulshan Kumar factor, etc., have played a positive role in the tourism development in the region.

10. In summers, Jammu city has little attraction for tourists.

11. Tourist resorts are scattered throughout the region, which is mostly hilly with poor infra-structural facilities.

Tourism Product of the Region – Bird's-Eye View

Tourism product for the tourist covers the complete experience, from the time he leaves his home till the time he returns back. In the case of tourism product, the basic raw materials would be the region's natural beauty, climate, history, culture and its people. Other aspects would be the existing facilities necessary for comfortable living such as water supply, electricity, roads, transport, communications and the other essentials. In other words, the tourism product can be seen as a composite product, as the sum total of the region's tourist attractions, transport, accommodation and entertainment which results in consumer satisfaction. The tourism product of the region is man-made as well as nature creation improved upon by man. The tourism product of the region is and contribution composite product, whether it is sold as a package or assembled by the individual tourist himself or his travel agent.

The tourism product of the region can, therefore, be analysed in terms of:

i)   Attractions of the region.

ii)   Facilities in the region.

iii) Accessibility to the region.

Attractions of the Region

Attractions are those elements in the tourism product which determine the choice of a particular tourist to visit one particular destination rather than another. These attractions facilitate the tourists to be motivated to visit a particular place. Few of the attractions of the region are:

1)   Interesting places

    a)   Jammu

    b)   Kud

    c)   Patnitop

    d)   Sanasar

    e)   Batote

    f)   Bhadarwah

    g)   Kishtwar

    h)   Akhnoor

    i)   Maeshedi

    j)   Reasi

    k)   Poonch

l) Noori-cham

m) Bani, Sarthal

n) Thana Mandi

o) Mandi and Loren

p) Behram Gala and Dera Gala

q) Mendhar Valley

r) Rajouri

s) Sudh Mahadey

t) Lal Draman and Dal Draman

u) Chenani

v) Paddar

w) Panchari

x) Jajjar Kotli

y) Mantalai

z) Lati, Jai, Padari, SEOJ, etc.

2. Holy places

a) Shri Mata Vaishno Devi cave

b) Aghar Jitto

c) Shiv Khori

d) Shahadara Shrief

e) Buddha Amarnath

f) Sudh Maha Dev temple

g) Sukhrala Devi

h) Purmandal and Uttar Bahni

i) Devika

j) Tombs of Baba Farid-ud-din and Issar-ud-din sahib

k) Fingla Devi

l) Baba Jitto (Jhiri)

m) Sarthal Devi

n) Chhechhi Devi

o) Kol Khondoli

p) Baba Pahar

q) Kaplas Kund

r) Dera Baha

s) Dera Baha Benda Sahib

t) Numerous temples in Jammu city and around

u) Maha Maya temple

v) Bahwe wali Mata

w) Pirmitha, Pir Roshan Shah wali, Pir Budan Ali Shah, Panch Pir, etc.

x) Pir khoh

y) Smadhi Maharani Chand Kaur

3. Ancient monuments

a) Kirimchi temples

b) Babor temple

c) Ruins of the old palaces in Basohli

d) Mahabilishwar Shiva temple in Billawar

e) Rangmahal in Ramnagar

f) Palace of Zorawar Singh Reasi

g) Mubarak Mandi palace

h) Mahor-Garh

i) Akhnoor excavation

j) Poni

k) Jama Massid Rajouri

l) Chingas sarai

m) Gajapat fort

n) Bhim garh fort

o) Poonch fort

p) Fort-cum sarai Nawshera

q) Bahu fort

r) Amrbaran

s) Bhadarwah fort, etc.

4. Lakes

a) Mansar Lake

b) Surinsar Lake

c) Kaplas Lake

d) Lakes in Poonch area

5. Rivers

i) The Chenab

ii) The Ravi

iii) The Tawi

6. Trekking, Mountaineering and Expedition

7. Sports attractions

8. Gliding, skiing, golf, etc.

9. Dreamland at Katra, Revolving Restaurant at Jammu

10. Amar Manal Museum

11. Dogra Art Gallery

12. Bag-E-Bahu

13. Bhadarwahi Rajmash, Dry fruit, Basmati rice, Kashmiri shawls and handicrafts, etc.

Facilities in the Region

Accommodation facilities are available at almost all places; however, they may be inadequate at some places. Various types of entertainment, picnic sites, recreation, etc., are also available although in a limited way. Dhaba culture is dominating in food industry.

Accessibility

For an adventure tourist, all areas in the region are accessible. The region is hilly, connected with other parts of the country by means of rail, road and air. Efficiency of the transport system and tourist satisfaction in the region may have some question marks. Few of the tourist attractions in the region which are located at places where there are no transport facilities or where there are inadequate transport facilities, have little value.

OBJECTIVES OF TOURISM DEVELOPMENT IN THE REGION

Fundamentally, the objective of tourism development in the region is economic one. Deprived from other natural resources for its development, the state of Jammu and Kashmir has little option but for depending heavily on tourism as a means of its development. Tourism in the region has become an industry. It regenerates as it pollutes, pays off as it undermines its very base, represents a source both of constructive experience and cultural enrichment as of alienation and degradation.

With its rich tourism product, the region has excellent perspective for its development. In future, the tourism industry in the region can become a strong economic force if it is understood by the persons involved in its totality. This requires not only the understanding of phenomenon, but a commitment to achieve the objectives. The support of the state government should be visible and demonstrative. For better understanding of the subject, it is required that the problems faced by the industry in the region are properly understood and provide some possible suggestion to improve the lot of tourism industry.

PROBLEMS AND SUGGESTIONS

Problems

Few of the problems faced by the tourism industry in the region are as under:

1. **Mismanagement:** The overall giant of tourism planning activities are grapping with managerial chaos. Planning work is not undertaken scientifically and systematically. Plans are prepared in a haphazard manner by the bureaucrats and politicians when in power rather than by economists, scientists and experts. Often it happens that ambitious schemes are planned and launched in the region without much reference to the return on capital invested, economic viability and availability of the related infrastructure.

The tourism product of the region has been commercialised and merchandised to the outside world in a limited manner and that too only in recent times. Due to serious lapses in the marketing research, it has been difficult to identify the problematic areas in the tourism industry. No service efforts have ever been made to approach the new markets where the potential tourists are readily available.

2. *Problems of Infrastructure Facilities:* Inadequate infrastructure facilities are the major bottlenecks retarding the tourist traffic in the region. Inadequate accommodation, long journey in uncomfortable buses on uneven roads, etc. add to the problems of tourism agencies and highlight the need to develop infrastructure facilities. In an opinions survey conducted by the author among different categories of tourists, it was found that the reasons for unsatisfactory travel were bad roads, over crowdedness, uncomfortable seats, no availability of reservation in time, unhealthy eating places en route, non-cooperative behaviour of the transport people, etc.

3. *Tourist Traffic at Few Places:* Tourist traffic in the region is mainly to Shri Mata Vaishno Devi cave. Very few tourists from outside the state visit other places in the region.

4. *Growing Competition from Neighboring Places:* Kashmir valley and Ladakh region are competitors within the state. In recent years, competition from the neighbouring places like Himachal Pradesh and Haryana has increased.

5. *Terrorism Within the State:* Potential tourists have shifted their destination from the region to elsewhere due to growing terrorism activities in the State. Since safety of the tourist is threatened, he is no more interested to make the adventure, risking his own life for nothing. Whether there is any disruptive activity, either by the terrorists or by the local people, tourist's abstain from the place. Strikes, bandhs,

231

etc. also affect the smooth development of the tourism industry.

6. **Behaviour of the People:** People in the region have displayed unforgettable hospitality in the past. Modern tourists expect high quality treatment, which they seldom receive now. Behaviour of the people involved in the tourism industry is not upto the expectations of the visitors.

7. **Lack of Positive Demonstration Effect:** Many tourists leave the region with very negative impression, which is sure to create trouble in the future against the healthier development of tourism industry in the region.

8. **Natural Factors:** The climate of the region is quite varied because of its location and topography. During one day's journey, one may find different types of climate. Temperature variations over space and time are also recorded to extreme limits. Therefore, these natural factors have further increased the hurdles in the smooth development of tourism industry in the region. In rainy and winter season, roads get blocked due to heavy landslides, which creates problems for the tourist to travel from one place to another.

9. **Malpractices:** Cheating and other such malpractices by the persons engaged in tourism industry in the region are further putting restrictions in the path of healthy development of tourism in the region. Since there is no strong agency to control these malpractices tourist does not enter or leave the region in a happy and confident mood. Maltreatment, which a tourist receives at the hands of rickshaw drivers, hotel owners, etc. is unforgettable. Arbitrary rates are charged from the tourists.

10. **Poor Publicity:** A penetrating approach with high imagination and a professional touch is lacking in the publicity programme of the tourism department and tourist industry in the region.

Very few modern techniques of publicity are being used for this purpose.

11. **Lack of Research:** Surprisingly, there is no research wing in the tourism department. No serious thought has ever been given to this crucial aspect of the industry. Without knowing what a tourist wants, all efforts of the State Government are futile.

12. **Absence of Tourism Education:** One of the prerequisites for the successful development of tourism lies in the professionals taking charge of the industry from the untrained and non-professionals. In the region in particular and state in general no efforts have been made to develop trained human resource to mange the tourism industry. The lack of tourism education in the region has thrown the tourism industry in the hands of short-term profit seekers destroying the long-term prospect of the tourism product of the region.

Suggestions

Due to above stated problem, it becomes a matter of great concern to determine the policy for the promotion of tourism in the region.

1. **Sound Tourism Planning:** The haphazard development of tourism industry in the region needs planning of the industry on scientific lines. Tourism planning should not be left to private enterprises in search of profit. Government must actively participate in it. The strategy for planning of tourism is required to be framed at all levels, i.e. regional, city and village. Each tourist resort of the region should be so explored, after thorough microgeographic examination, that it may present a profile of prospects and may contribute to the total image of the region.

2. **Organisation:** There should be a Tourism Development Council for the region in which the representatives of

Central Government, State Government, private agencies in tourism sector and experts be involved in chalking out the programme and policy for tourism development in the region.

At execution level, there may be a Tourism Executive Committee and a Monitoring cell which should collect the needed data regarding the performance in different sectors of the industry. The result of the periodic performance appraisal should be sent to take suitable measures to ward off all exigencies of deviation from the desired course of action.

3. *Effective Marketing:* How to sell the region's tourism and pilgrim products in the modern competitive markets is a major question?

The State's Department of Tourism must associate all prominent private sector tourism enterprises, Shri Mata Vaishno Devi Shrine Board, through word-of-mouth, i.e. JKTDC travel agencies and other related agencies in chalking out the tourism marketing strategies to make them broad-based and more result oriented because these private travel agencies do bulk of tourism marketing. Their representatives should be included in a committee for marketing purposes. The best tourism marketing strategy for the region may be what the tourists who have sojourned and enjoyed the reception given to them say about it afterwards. By word of mouth, they can make or break the region's reputation. The impact of this spontaneous propaganda will either reinforce or cancel out the results from governmental publicity. There is no substitute for a well-satisfied customer in the marketing strategy.

4. *Development of Transport Facilities:* Internal transport is the starting point of planning for growth of tourist traffic. Internal transport plays a pivotal role in the development of tourism

industry. Inefficient transport is the main obstacle in the development of tourism. A reappraisal of the transport systems is required. Indian Railways should think and implement a plan to take the railway to Katra, the base camp of Mata Vaishno Devi cave. Increased pilgrim traffic in coming future need a four-lane National highway upto Katra. There is a needs to establish air transport, cable ropeway, etc. in the region. On the roadside, no eating place should come up without having proper parking place.

5. *Development of Boarding and Lodging Facilities:* A master plan for the development of boarding and lodging facilities should be chalked out for the region. Due to Article 370 in operation, none of the big business houses have ever thought of setting up boarding and lodging places in the State. Only Mr Gulshan Kumar's boarding places in shape of langers are functional in the region. Some type of relaxation and concession should be provided to interested parties to invest and construct accommodation/eating places either free of cost or at subsidised rates. This may go a big way to attract economic class of tourists/pilgrims.

Catering services in the State are very poor. Hygienically very poor quality food is served to the economic class tourists which needs immediate corrective treatment. Food served en route to different tourists is of very poor nature. Education of personnel involved in catering services and strict quality control is suggested. Nowhere in the region Dogri food is served. In catering, the region should identify itself with the Dogri food. In eating places, instead of serving the Bhadarwani Rajmash, cheap quality Rajmash are cooked and served.

6. *Development of Tourist Resort:* Apart from Shri Mata Vaishno Devi Shrine and Patnitop, Government should develop other places in the region, which provide charm and add to the variety. Bani, Sarthal, Bhadarwah, Kishtwar,

Poonch, Rajouri, Ramnagar, Mantalai, Sudhmahadev, Lalti, Dudu, Basantgarh, Machedi, Panchari, Sanasar and other such areas if developed are full of tourism potential. These places should be provided with minimum resort facilities at first instance and then developing full facilities later on.

7. **Enriching En route Facilities:** En route facilities in the region are not up to the mark. Facilities created by the JKTDC attract a small lot. These places should be given to private agencies on contractual basis. These agencies have their own ways to generate profits which the public sector enterprises are unable to do. Need is to have a system to check the quality in this case.

8. **Hotels Construction:** Since the pilgrim traffic has indicated sign of rapid growth in the region, construction activities have expanded without any orderly urban development. Extension of construction activities near the tourist resorts if not properly regulated, may spoil the scenic beauty of the area. Therefore, it is suggested that Government should implement master plans for the development of main tourist resorts, which is hoped to provide relief in the congested areas, improve sanitary conditions, earmark areas for building and preserve the essential attractive characteristics of the centres from the tourist point of view.

9. **Checking Malpractices:** Enforcement of the Jammu and Kashmir Registration of Tourist Trade Act 1975 is very poor. The implementation of the Act needs to be strict to effectively check the malpractices. A special squad of honest policemen should be charged with attending any such complaint and also prohibit begging outside the hotels, railway platforms, near restaurants, on main roads, temples and other tourist places.

10 **Tourism Education:** So much of talk on tourism without proper tourism education is going to help in a little way. There is strong need to have a force of people who are well

versed with the intricacies of the tourism trade. For this, it is suggested that a course be introduced at all stages of education in the State. Moreover, Bachelor and Master degree programmes on tourism be started in the State.

11. *Tourism Research:* On account of its incalculable benefits, research is considered as a precondition for planning. But it is really surprising that there is no arrangement of tourism research in the State and nothing is earmarked for the said purpose. It is suggested that at least two tourism research centres – one with the help of Mata Vaishno Devi Shrine Board and other by the State Tourism Department should come up for undertaking in-depth research on the subject.

12. *Recreational Facilities:* Recreation facilities in the region are few. Dreamland Park at Katra Bagh – Bahu, revolving restaurant at Jammu are of very recent origin. The region needs more recreational facilities in the shape of artificial lake in and around Jammu city, Zoo museum, sanctuary, parks, gardens, clubs, sports, Yoga centres, cultural programmes, etc.

13. *Other Suggestions:*

   a)   Changing Jhiri fare on the lines of Pushkar mela.

   b)   Developing pilgrimage circuit such as Kol Khondali-Vaishno Devi – Agar Jitto-Shiv Khori- Shahadara Shrief- Budha Amarnath Baba Jitto (Jhiri)- Bhawe wali Mata.

   OR

   Vaishno Devi – Devika- Sudh Mahadev-Mantalai-Sukhrala Devi- Mansar-Chechi Mata.

   c)   Developing mixed circuit of pilgrimage-cum-tourism, like Vaishno Devi- Patnitop- danasar-Surinsar-Manasar.

   d)   Developing Mantalai as sports and Yoga centre.

e) More shopping facilities.

f) Identification, presentation and development of historical places and monuments.

g) Begging be declared as punishable crime.

h) Insurance of tourists.

i) Instilling civic sense.

j) Checking crime and terrorism.

k) Creation of tourist villages.

l) Small tourist villages with complete facilities.

m) Package tour.

n) Hotels should develop and categorised on the basis of environment maintenance.

CONCLUSION

Pilgrimage is a significant activity of the region. Little has been done for the promotion of tourism industry in the past and a great deal of effort is required to boost tourism in the region. There is need to educate the public on the merits and demerits of tourism in the region in general and in particular develop a force of training personnel who have to deal with the tourist directly.

REFERENCES

1. A.K. Bhatia, 1991, *International Tourism Fundamentals and Practices*, Sterling Publishers Private Limited, New Delhi.

2. A.P. Singh, 1989, *Himalayan Environment and Tourism*, Chugh Publications, Allahabad.

3. Desh Bandhu, 1989, *Jammu Kashmir*, and Ladakh, Akashdeep Publishing House, Delhi.

4. Desh Bandhu, 1983, *Income and Employment Effects of Tourism – A Case Study of Jammu Kashmir* (Unpublished Ph.D. thesis). University of Jammu, Jammu.

5. Georgis Hooton, 1982, *Introduction to Resort Management*, Nelson Hall, Chicago.

6. J.C. Hclloway. & R.V. Plant, 1990, *Marketing for Tourism*, Pitman Publishing. London.

7. Marie-Francoise lanfant, 1980, *Introduction Tourism in the Process of Internationalisation*, International Social Science Journal. XXXII, (1), pp. 14-43.

8. Peter Lengyel, 1980, *Editorial*, International Social Sciences Journal, XXXII, (1), pp. 7-13.

9. Richard England, 1980, *Architecture for tourists*, International Social Science Journal, XXXII, (1), pp. 44-55.

TOURISM EDUCATION IN THE 21ST CENTURY: CHALLENGES AND OPPORTUNITY

S K GUPTA*

Tourism is a major social phenomenon of the modern society with enormous economic consequences. Its importance as an instrument for economic development and employment generation, particularly in remote and backward areas, has been now well recognised the world over. Promotion of the tourism sector *per se* generates a plethora of both economic and social benefits: GDP, employment generation, foreign exchange earning, infrastructure development, investments, rural development, conservation of naturals and promotion of social integration and international understanding across countries.

Tourism is the world's largest export industry today. According to World Tourism Organisation in 1998, 625 million

* Department of Tourism, H.N.B. Garhwal University.

tourists travelled internationally and spent about 445 US $ billion in places visited by them. International travel receipts and passenger transport amounted to more than US $ 504 billion, putting it ahead of all other categories of international trade. Over the past 15 years international tourism receipts have grown 1.5 times faster than the world GDP, with no sign of slowing down in the future. International tourism is just the tip of the iceberg in comparison to domestic tourism. WTO estimates the total size of international and domestic tourism in 1998 to be more than 3 billion travellers with revenues topping US $ 1.7 trillion. International tourism accounted for an estimated 8 per cent of the world's total export earnings and 37 per cent of export in service sector. In 1997, travel and tourism was expected to provide direct and indirect employment to 255 million people and accounted for about 11% of global workforce. It is estimated that there are 115 million direct tourism jobs worldwide which is approximately 4 per cent of the world total. Millions of more indirect jobs can be attributed to the tourism sector through the ripple affect it creates on the economy. Only a small part of tourism spending occurs in what are normally considered tourism industries, businesses such as travel agencies or hotels. A very large part of tourism consumption takes place outside the tourism industries in public and private services, such as buses and metro systems, museums, also retail shops, etc. Hence the direct and indirect employments which result from tourism are:

► People involved in providing travel and tourism services to consumers, business travellers and government travellers such as airline personnel, hotel personnel, car rental agents, tour operators and travel agents and retail merchants.

► People involved in buildings, equipments and suppliers like hotels and resorts, aircrafts, automobiles and food/ beverages.

► People involved in providing government travel and tourism services such as tourism promotion offices, park services, etc.

Looking at the trends of international tourist arrivals during the decade 1989-98, the growth rate of arrivals worldwide slowed in the second half of the decade to 3.2 per cent from 5 per cent in the first half. For the ten-year period 1989-98 overall, the annual average was 4.3 per cent. The regions which are likely to experience the maximum growth in tourist traffic in the coming years are East Asia/ Pacific and South Asia. The factor which is favourable to South Asia region includes strong growth of tourism due to the economic liberalisation programme in India and the consequent foreign investment opportunities, development of tourist facilities including expansion of airline services, etc.

TOURISM IN INDIA AND ITS EMPLOYMENT POTENTIAL

India received a mere 16,829 international tourists in 1951. The arrivals increased to 2.40 million in 1997 and registered a compound annual rate of growth of about 11.5%. Though it is a remarkable progress, it is still below our potentials. Considering the geographical size of the country and the diversity of attractions, the share of India in the world tourist traffic is still about 0.4%. However, the mainstay of Indian tourism is domestic tourism. According to figures available from the State Governments, about 156 million domestic tourists stayed in the paid accommodation units during 1997 and in addition it is expected that there would have been about 150 million pilgrim tourists who did not use paid accommodation. Presently, tourism is India's third largest industry after ready-made garments and gem and jewellery.

The foreign exchange earning from tourism during 1998-99 is estimated to be Rs 11540 crores. In 1997 tourism economy contributed an estimated Rs 904.6 billion accounting for 5.6% of India GDP (WTTC) as compared to world average of 10% of GDP. The most significant feature of the tourism industry is its capacity to generate large-scale employment opportunities particularly in remote and backward areas. A desirable feature of tourism industry is that it employs a large number of women, both educated and uneducated. The Economic and Social Commission for Asia and Pacific (ESCAP) study report on 'Economic Impact of Tourism in India' revealed that a visit by 1.2 international tourists provides employment to one person per year while 17 domestic tourists generate employment for one person. By using these ratios and projections of tourist traffic, the forecast of direct employment in the tourism sector during the Ninth Plan period have been worked out.

FORECASTS OF DIRECT EMPLOYMENT IN THE TOURISM SECTOR DURING NINTH PLAN PERIOD

Year	Employment Generation (Millions)		
	Trend Estimated	Modified Estimate	NAPT Projection
1996-97	9.15	9.19	9.44
1997-98	9.91	9.99	10.48
1998-99	10.81	10.92	11.74
1999-00	11.77	11.93	12.96
2000-01	12.80	13.00	14.17

Source: Report of the Working Group on Tourism for the Ninth Plan, June 1996, Dept. of Tourism, Ministry of Civil Aviation & Tourism, Govt. of India, New Delhi.

In 1997, the direct employment in this sector was about 10 million and the indirect employment was another 21.5 million people. According to WTTC, by 2010 tourism industry will support 25 million direct jobs, which will be 6.8% of total employment. Labour-Capital ratio per million rupee of investment at 1985-86 prices is 47.5 in tourism and is as high as 89 jobs in hotels and restaurants compared to 44.7 jobs in agriculture and a mere 12.7 in the manufacturing sector. This indicates the labour intensive nature of jobs created by tourism and related activities. The employment multiplier in the tourism is 2.36, i.e. direct employment of one person in the tourism industry creates jobs for

1.36 persons in other sectors of the economy. Hence sufficient human resources in all categories of tourism industry would be required to meet the demand of 3 million international tourists. The realisation of the employment potential would, however, depend on the extent to which the education and training imparted by the public and private sector in tourism is integrated to the various employment generation schemes of the Central and the State government.

TOURISM EDUCATION AND TRAINING IN INDIA

People engaged in the tourism trade create experiences, good or bad. The quality and efficiency of service is the primary concern of the tourism industry. In order to achieve that, each of the components of tourism industry requires trained/skilled manpower. The airlines need highly trained air hostesses and a host of technicians. The immigration officers at the airports need to be smart, personable and capable of handling other security and public relations functions efficiently. The taxi drivers, coast operators and other grass roots level workers need to be trained to behave well with the tourists. Training is also to be imparted to guides, to watch and ward staff at monuments, wildlife sanctuaries, etc., to make them more responsive to the tourists. But hotels and restaurants, travel agents, tour operators and other providers of tourist services need professionally trained manpower at all levels from front line staff to supervisory, lower and middle level managerial staff and senior managers. Development of human resources is thus a major activity in the promotion of tourism. Manpower development for tourism industry at present includes mainly two activities:

(i)   Training and education in accommodation sector.

(ii) Training and education in travel trade.

Training and Education in Accommodation Sector

In the accommodation and hospitality sector, the training programmes are broadly of two types. The first is the statutory apprenticeship programme for certain categories of trades like stewards, housekeeping staff, cooks, front office personnel and the like. The second one is the formal structured programme offered by the institutions set up by the Government at the craft and diploma levels. The Hotel Management and Catering Technology institutes and Food Craft institutes of Government of India provide training in different aspects of hotel and catering operations at supervisory, middle management and craft levels. At present, there are 21 of Hotel Management institutes offering a 3-year diploma course in hotel management and catering technology and the craft level institutions offer courses of 6 months to one year duration in various food crafts such as: cookery, bakery and confectionery; restaurant and counter service; hotel reception and bookkeeping, housekeeping; canning and food preservation etc. Apart from 3 years Diploma programme, the Hotel Management institutes also offer various craft courses. To infuse certain specialisation, postgraduate courses in hotel administration and food production of duration of 18 months are also available in selected institutes. The expected annual turn-out of these institutes till 2000 AD is given in Table below:

ANNUAL TURN-OUT OF INSTITUTES

Course	Number of Students					
	1995	1996	1997	1998	1999	2000
Three Year Diploma	900	1200	1400	1800	2200	2400
P.G. Courses	200	450	500	500	500	500
Craft Courses	505	600	600	600	900	1100
Total	1605	2250	2500	2900	3600	4000

Sources: Report of the working group on Tourism for the Ninth Five Year Plan, June 1996, Dept. of tourism, Ministry of Civil Aviation & Tourism, Govt. of India, New Delhi.

For effective coordination of the various training programmes available in the field of hotel management and catering technology, the Government of India has set up the National Council for Hotel Management and Catering Technology as an apex body under the Ministry of Tourism and Civil Aviation. The primary objectives of the Council are:

▶ To provide well trained professionals to meet the growing requirements of the industry by organising programmes at management, supervisory and craft levels.

▶ To act as the main policy making body for this purpose and function as a professional body conducting examinations and conferring recognitions and accreditation of professional merit.

▶ To standardise courses and infrastructure requirements.

▶ To play a key role in creating a modern and model hospitality education training system in India to meet the varied and changing requirements of manpower for the Indian industry and to meet the challenges of international technological development.

▶ To prescribe educational and other qualifications along with experience, etc. for members of staff in the affiliated institutions and introduce faculty development programmes.

The Central Apprenticeship Councils set up at Delhi, Faridabad and Meerut by the Ministry of Labour under the Central Apprenticeship Act provide training in cooking, bakery and confectionery, stewardship and housekeeping. The annual output of these centres is about 1600 trainees. There are also a few craft level institutes run by the State Governments. These institutes turn out about 250 persons every year. Besides, several universities are also running Bachelor of Hotel Management programmes. In private sector some of the major hotel chains run their own training institutes in hotel management and catering technology and these include:

i) School of Hotel Administration, Manipal (100 trainees)

ii) Indian Institute of Hotel Management, Aurangabad (Taj Group, 60 trainees).

iii) Oberoi School of Hotel Management, Delhi (40 trainees)

iv) Academy of Culinary Education, Chided de Goa Beach Resort, Goa

The universities of Madras and Bangalore have affiliated several catering institutes which award Bachelor's degree in Hotel Management. The approximate annual turnout of these institutes would be around 500 students. There are also about 35 private institutes conducting training courses in hospitality and catering. Most of them conduct 3 year diploma programmes and award their own diplomas. Some of them are recognised by AICTE and about 500 students had graduated from these institutes by 1997. There are also some other institutes which have tie-ups with American Hotel and Motel Association or Swiss Hotel Schools. These institutes turn out about 250 students every year. The total turnout of all the hotel and catering technology schools in India is thus about 5000 students per year. As against this, the actual requirement per year is about 20,000 persons, assuming that one additional room would require at least one trained person. There is, thus, going to be a wide gap between the supply and demand in the trained manpower in the hotel management and catering technology sector. Though the gap between demand and supply is likely to be met by the private institutes to a large extent, the Government institutes have to play a major role in maintaining the standards of education. These institutes should also be able to meet the aspirations of students who cannot afford to pay the fees and other expenses charged by the private institutes. It is particularly so in the case of less developed areas. There are no post graduate courses in Hotel Management and Catering Technology presently available in India. As a result, the professional staff in the IHMS and Food Craft Institutes in India does not have any opportunity to acquire higher qualifications. It is, therefore, absolutely necessary to set up an Institute of Advanced Hotel Management offering postgraduate courses. The National Council for Hotel Management and Catering Technology needs to be strengthened to standardise the course material and accredit private institutes. Formulation of competency standards and certification on the basis of these standards also would be necessary to bring out qualitative improvements in the existing stock of personnel in the tourism industry.

Under the technical assistance of European Commission, a South Asia Integrated Tourism Human Resource Development project (SA-ITHRDP) has been taken up. National occupational skill standards have been specified for 8 occupations – 5 on the hospitality side and 3 on the travel and tourism side – under the project. Training programmes for the trainers have been started to make them aware of the standards. These competency standards are proposed to be updated on a continuous basis.

Training and Education in Tourism and Travel Trade

The decade of 1980s was a pivotal one for tourism and hospitality education. As we entered the decade, tourism was still struggling for recognition as a major socio-economic force, tourism education was still largely ignored as essential to the well-being of what would soon become the world's largest industry. As a consequence, formal attention being paid to tourism education focussed largely on the many problems facing the field. And there were only a few organisations, associations or forums within which the issues related to tourism education could be raised and debated and therefore, there seemed little scope for the emergence of any major institutions imparting education and training in allied fields. At university level, only Delhi University established its tourism course in 1972 as part of BA Vocational Studies Programme, without any permanent faculty members.

However, as we entered the 1990s, radically different picture emerged. Tourism education and training was accorded recognition and even priority by a significant number of governments and educational institutions. The whole industry awakened to the fact that existing efforts to provide training for frontline staff and supervisors must be balanced by education programmes for present and future managers, so as to ensure, among other things, that the trained personnel are deployed and utilised effectively.

The Indian Institute of Tourism and Travel Management (IITTM) established by the Ministry of Tourism in January 1983, has been a major development in the field of professionalisation of tourist services. It has signified the new awareness and importance attached to tourism education and training. However, in India, tourism education achieved a significant progress after the formation of National Committee on Tourism (NCT) in 1988. The NCT examined the entire issue of human resources development and found several weaknesses both in qualitative and quantitative dimensions. The NCT in its report to the Government recommended the following:

▶ IITTM should be effectively developed to enable it to perform its assigned role. It will have, in due course, regional centres so that tourism becomes a broad based, recognised discipline of education.

▶ It should be reconstituted by a resolution of the Government to enable it to function effectively as an apex body in tourism education development and to empower it to award diplomas and degrees.

▶ Full-time management courses should be taken up in the existing universities.

The National Action Plan for Tourism announced in May 1992 also states that:

The IITTM will be strengthened in staff and equipment to become the premier institution for providing trained manpower for the travel in the country. National universities will also be involved in the effort and would be given financial and other assistance for introducing tourism courses in the country.

IITTM and its Role

During 1987-88 the institute launched a unique series of six Management Development Programmes (MDP) on the Open University pattern. These MDPs were the first of their kind in the country and have fulfilled a long felt need of travel industry for upgrading the professional skills by providing formal tourism qualification to professionals in the industry as also to those aspiring to join it. The courses are conducted on a cyclic basis. The MDP programmes offer participants the choice of affording one or more of these courses to earn a certificate (3MDPS) or diploma (5 MDPS) in tourism management. As a result of institute's initiatives, 1989 heralded an unprecedented development in tourism courses at postgraduate level. For the first time the institute developed the syllabus for the Master Degree in Tourism Administration (MTA) which was considered and adopted at the National Workshop of Educationists on Manpower Development for Tourism Sector, held in October 1988. With this, tourism at postgraduate degree and postgraduate diploma level was introduced in various universities like Kurukshetra, Garwhal, Indore, Gwalior, Aligarh, Shimla, Jodhpur, Pondicherry, Bilaspur, Vellore, Aurangabad, Tirupati, Pune, Banaras Hindu University, Jhashi, Kumaon, etc. More and more universities are prepared to introduce these courses. Besides, at the graduate level, tourism and hotel management courses have also been introduced in various universities and government colleges. Moreover, tourism administration/management has also been included as a subject in National Education Test (NET) by the University Grants Commission (UGC) for Junior Research Fellowship and eligibility for lectureship in year 2000.

From the academic year 1995-96, IITTM has started full-time courses in Tourism Management (14 months) and Destination Management (8 months) at Gwalior.

The IITTM and its chapters have a mandate to produce trained manpower for the travel industry. It is also having the responsibility of imparting training to Central and state Government offices involved in tourism development, training of industry personnel and grass roots level workers like immigration officers, taxi drivers, guides, etc. The courses presently being run by the institute include:

i)   Part-time Management Development Programmes.

ii)   Diploma in Travel and Tourism Industry Management.

iii) Language training programmes in French, German, Spanish, Japanese, etc.

iv)   Training for grass roots level workers.

During Ninth Plan, it is proposed to enlarge the activities of IITTM and its chapters to include:

i)   MBA (Tourism Management)

ii)   Diploma in Tourism Marketing Management

iii) Faculty exchange and faculty enrichment programmes through training in India and abroad.

iv)   Student exchange programme.

v)   Setting up audio-visual training facility.

IITTM has its branch at Bhubaneswar and it is also proposed to set up two branches of IITTM (one each in south and west) and to give it the status of a deemed university. IITTM has to become a model institute for tourism training with all the necessary infrastructure and equipments.

National Institute of Water Sports

The Institute was set up at Goa in 1990 to promote sports activities in the country. The Institute is presently working under the administrative control of IITTM. The Government of Goa has provided land for the construction of building for the Institute. It needs to be constructed and plans to expand its activities during the Plan period.

Institute of Skiing and Mountaineering

The Institute at Glummer was set up in 1968 to provide training in adventure sports such as skiing, mountaineering, rock climbing, etc. It is now proposed to be handed over to the State Government for its continued operation. It is also proposed to establish similar facilities at Auli (UP) and Simla (HP) under the Central Government for giving further impetus to adventure tourism.

Guide Training

The availability of trained guides in tourist centres and monuments is a major requirement for tourism promotion. The Department of Tourism is, therefore, giving considerable importance to guide training. A three-tier training programme at the national, state and local levels has recently been drawn up and is being implemented through Government of India Tourist offices, State Government and others. These courses include programmes for fresh tourist guides, language courses and refresher courses for those already engaged in the guide services.

IATA/UFTAA/FIATA's Training Programme

The International Air Transport Association (IATA) along with Universal Federation of Travel Agent Association (UFTAA) has designed training courses for travel consultants who work in IATA accredited travel agencies, personnel of airlines, general sales agents, and people who wish to work in a travel agency and their main task is to sell international air transportation on behalf of

IATA members airlines. The IATA/UFTAA International Travel Agents Training Programme offered through IATA Learning Centre (ILC) is available worldwide. The IATA/UFTAA diploma has gained industry recognition as a quality qualification important for any one wishing to upgrade his/her professional competence or start a career in the travel industry. The training programme is administered by local coordinators who are responsible for the promotion of the courses, the supply of training kit and the organisation of the examinations. The training courses can be taken as self-teach modules, and are also offered alternatively as classroom courses in more than 200 training establishments known as IATA/UFTAA authorised training centres located in many countries.

There are two types of courses:

▶ IATA/UFTAA International Travel Agents standard courses.

▶ IATA/UFTAA International Travel Agents advanced courses.

International Air Transport Association (IATA) along with International Federation of Freight Forwards Association (FIATA) has been conducting courses in air cargo. There are three types of courses offered by IATA-FIATA as follows:

▶ The introductory courses for new entrants in the field to understand basic cargo ratings and documentation procedure, i.e. completion of airwaybill.

▶ The International Air Cargo Rating courses which include consolidation and ULD (Unit Load Devices) calculations including freight calculations using rate construction and rate combination points – an advanced course for those already well versed in basic freight calculations.

▶ The prestigious Dangerous Goods course (DGR) helps to understand the legal aspects and responsibilities of the shippers, agents and airlines involved in the transport of dangerous goods and apply dangerous goods regulations correctly including packing, marketing, labelling, checking of declarations and delivering consignments to airlines ready for carriage.

DGR diploma holders are widely sought after in the industry because one of the prerequisites of having an air cargo agency accredited by IATA is to have a minimum of two employees who hold the DGR diploma or an IATA-FIATA diploma. Formerly, to acquire the above mentioned qualifications, one had to directly register with IATA by paying the course fees in Swiss Francs and obtain course material from them and prepare for examinations. However, since December 1994, IATA-FIATA have appointed IATA-FIATA authorised training centre in Mumbai to enable new entrants to register as well as get coaching and prepare for the IATA-FIATA examinations. So now it is not only possible to register with IATA but also to avail of coaching facilities for the examinations.

TOURISM EDUCATION AND GLOBALISATION

The accelerating trend towards the globalisation of products, services and markets necessarily also affects education, training and academic research in tourism. On the one hand, it is a process generated by the knowledge of industry itself, while on the other there is no doubt that the very dynamics of tourism activity require a commensurate response in developing knowledge in the sector. The traditional paradigm of knowledge acquisition in tourism implied – it should be recognised – a certain amount of improvisation resulting from the rapid growth of markets and the absence of an in-depth analysis of the medium and long-term needs of the sector. However, since tourism is becoming more complex and competitive with key variables such as technology, consumer tastes, the aspirations of professionals and the normative-administrative settings evolving a new mentality – a new paradigm – is emerging in tourism education. This new paradigm must respond to the constant changes in the key variables of tourism and the pedagogic process. Among these are:

(i)   the super–segmentation of activities;

(ii)   the growing standardisation of curricular contents;

(iii) the necessary flexibility in tourism career paths;

(iv)   the new technologies in tourism and in the acquisition of knowledge;

(v)   the growing competition among education institutions and the demand for transparency in degrees awarded; and

(vi)   the need to increase productivity in knowledge acquisition processes.

Specifically, the new paradigm should meet the expectations of the principal clients of this new tourism economy: the employees, the professionals and the society as a whole. The employers need to count on professionals who have acquired – and can continue to acquire – strategic skills. They want adaptable human resources, team players to build and develop business cultures apt for competitivity and development. They are aware that to attract and retain this type of professional, it is not enough to pay high salaries it is also necessary to offer an interesting and creative working atmosphere. On their part, students and professionals – who should be perpetual students in their jobs – will come from a multi-cultural background, with diverse motivations and expectations, and be quite pragmatic in using their abilities. Nevertheless, this pragmatism should be accompanied by a great capacity for conceptualisation and the necessary flexibility to constantly adapt to changing situations and to propose business strategies for survival and development.

Finally, society as a whole is going to require education, training and knowledge acquisition in general increasingly to meet the present and future needs. There are presently two visions on the profound role of tourism; (I) that tourism is a private market activity and that its success automatically contributes to the well-being of societies: and (II) that tourism is an activity which implies a great deal of cooperation between the private and public sectors, and it is this type of framework that encourages the success to tourism and its efficient contribution to social development. Thus, both visions are compatible with the previously mentioned need for quality and efficiency in tourism education.

ROLE OF WORLD TOURISM ORGANISATION IN SEARCH OF EFFICIENT TOURISM EDUCATION

WTO has enlarged its education programme and gave it an entirely new approach. WTO's Human Resource Development programme has been redefined and WTO has been creating useful instruments for greatly varied tourism activity. These instruments – the Tourism Education Quality (TEDQUAL) certification; the Graduate Tourism Aptitude Test (GTAT) methodology; the Themis Foundation and the Education Council are available to all the members of the organisation firstly to the Governments and also to enterprises and institutions who are affiliate members. TEDQUAL analyses the demand side and GTAT monitors giving the supply and give the information of what the employer needs and what the employee has to offer, enabling WTO to pinpoint where there is lack of quality in education and training.

A. Graduate Tourism Aptitude Test (GTAT)

In an effort to raise the standards of tourism education worldwide, WTO has developed a comprehensive proficiency exam called

GTAT to certify tourism graduates. The GTAT is intended to level the playing field for tourism students at the hundreds of specialised tourism training centres all over the world by setting voluntary international standards for curriculum design and course content. The GTAT is a two day exam in which the first part consists of some 700 multiple choice questions and five case studies on sixty five different knowledge domains, ranging from accounting and business law to geography, health issues in tourism and, problem solving and computer literacy. The second part covers language proficiency and people skills. Advanced level tourism students or practitioners can take the test. The test is to be offered periodically at WTO's Education Centres network and other affiliated institutions worldwide. Passing the GTAT earns a certificate and the right to use the initials FT (Fellow in Tourism) Certification combined with three years work experience in the tourism sector earns the right to become a WTP (World Tourism Professional) and earn the right to use those initials. There will be a permanent register (data back) at WTO of FT's and WTP's. The GTAT is also intended to help garner more respect for tourism education and tourism graduates, putting them on an equal footing with graduates from other professional fields.

B. WTO Education Council

The education council consists of tourism education institutions who wish to belong to WTO in order to jointly develop tourism education and training strategies, programmes and products in collaboration with other institutions, the industry and tourism administration. Becoming a member of the WTO education council offers the following significant advantages:

1. To be a member of a global organisation specifically dedicated to tourism, with an explicit shared strategy in the area of education and training.

2. To use the logotypes promoting quality and efficiency in tourism education.

3. To benefit from the promotional activities of WTO and its Themis Foundation, through the dissemination of information and specific activities aimed at the institutions of the Education Council.

4. To have access to the use of WTO education programmes and products.

5. To participate along with other institutions of recognised prestige in a global process towards excellence in tourism education.

The education institutions who wish to join the WTO education council should:

1. Accredit that they are a teaching institution at either university or third-cycle vocational training level with permanent tourism education programmes and recognised prestige.

2. Request and pass a TEDQUAL quality audit or several of their tourism education programmes (Diploma, B.A. degree, post graduate, masters and/ or doctorate).

3. Upon passing the above mentioned quality audit, request the status of Affiliate member of the World Tourism Organisation, under the established conditions for the same. Logically, this requirement is not necessary for those institutions who are already Affiliate Members.

C. Ted Qual Certification Process

WTO has developed, through its Themis Foundation, the Ted Qual Certification System to contribute to the quality and efficiency of tourism education. The Ted Qual certification proposes a methodology and voluntary standards with universal scope to more clearly define the quality of tourism education systems. The Ted Qual Certification System is thus a quality assurance system for tourism education and training. All teaching institutions and corporations, whether public or private wishing to certify specific Tourism Education Programmes (TEPs) can voluntarily submit these programmes to this process. The specific aims of the Ted Qual Certification System are: (I) to establish a quality assurance model through voluntary standardisation of tourism education and training systems, and (II) to smoothen the way towards greater pedagogic productivity and efficiency in tourism. The Ted Qual certification process has clear-cut and well defined stages, all of which are necessary to effectively determine to what extent the requirements of the Ted Qual standards are fulfilled.

Request for Information

All teaching institutions wishing to certify their TEP (s) according to the criteria established by the Ted Qual certification system should make an application (in writing) to the WTO Themis Foundation. Once the application has been received, the WTO Themis Foundation will send, free of charge information concerning the Ted Qual Certification System along with a pre Registration form.

CONCLUSION

Tourism is the industry of the 21st century, but tourism education is its final frontier. The current system is suffering a paradigm paralysis and needs a profound change. Tourism education in the future will have to respond to permanent change and integrate new quality and efficiency methodologies. There is urgent need for upgrading teaching methods offering incentives to staff to take part in training programmes incorporating existing technology, and setting up a permanent training process. Now training methods will have to fulfill two apparently contradictory conditions-training staff for a specific job and at the same time, preparing them for greater mobility in the labour market. Current issues involved are:

▶ Improved coordination between employers and training institutions.

▶ Increased investment in tourism training.

▶ Seeking efficiency through new methods and technologies.

▶ The motivation and stimulation of those involved in tourism training.

Computer programmes and telecommunications will be key technologies in revolutionising tourism training by providing the basis for everything from long-distance interactive training and personalised teaching and evaluation programmes to create a Global Tourism Training Community of employers, professionals and educationists.

The key trends for the future are:

▶ A globalisation of training and increased international cooperation.

▶ Improved coordination and cooperation between the sub-sectors of tourism.

▶ A key role for research.

▶ More flexible training programmes.

▶ The need for staff to undergo continuous training.

The situation that is likely to emerge is that there should be sufficient people produced each year to meet the manpower needs of the tourism industry. There is a need for existing tourism courses at all levels to develop new models in tourism covering a broader spectrum of the tourism industry. Only in this way, the colleges, institutes and universities running tourism training programmes can begin to meet the long-term needs of the whole industry. Because of the present low level of penetration of technology in tourism, there is great potential for significant gains in performance and productivity, in both facility design and service delivery.

REFERENCES

Andrews, Sudhir (1994), India, Case Study of Human Resources in Tourism in Baum Tom (ed.), Human Resources Issues in International Tourism Butterworth-Heinemann, Oxford.

Annual Report (1999-2000), Ministry of Tourism, Government of India.

Bagri, S.C. (1997), *Tourism Education in India: Opportunities and Challenges* in Navin Mathur (ed.), International Journal of Management and Tourism, Volume 6, Number 2, October- December, 1997, Jodhpur.

Donald E. Hawkins and John D. Hunt (1987), *Travel and Tourism Professional Education* in Navin Mathur (ed.) International Journal of Management and Tourism; Vol. 1, No.3, January- March 1993.

Education and Training for Tourism (1987), World Tourism Organisation, General Assembly (Seventh Session, Agenda item- 15) Madrid.

ESCAP Tourism Newsletter, No. 4, August 1994, Bangkok.

Know India (1989), Ministry of Tourism and Civil Aviation, Government of India.

Lavery, P. (1987), *The Education Training and Manpower Needs of Tourist Industry* in Great Britain up to 1990 in T.V. Singh (ed.) Tourism Recreation Research, Vol. XII No.1, 1987 Lucknow.

Ted Qual, A WTO. Themis Publication, Noo. 2.1/2000, WTO.

WTO News 1997, WTO Madrid Issue 1, March 1997 WTO News 1997, Issue 4, October 1997, WTO, Madrid.

WTO News 1998, Issue 3, May – June 1998, WTO, Madrid.

MANPOWER DEVELOPMENT FOR TOURISM SECTOR IN INDIA

D S BHARDWAJ*
SIDDHARATHA SHANKAR**

INTRODUCTION

At present the wind is blowing in favour of liberalisation, globalisation, privatisation, MNCs, World Trade Organisation and so forth to boost the world's economy. Contrary to expectations the world economy has registered declining trends in various spheres in recent years. The IMF Survey rightly cautioned there were "significant downside risks" to the global outlook. In this gloomy economic scenario, tourism seems to be a ray of hope.

* Chairman & Dean, Tourism, Faculty of Commerce & Management, Kurukshetra University, Kurukshetra - 136 119.
** Lecturer in Management, Regional Centre, Jalandhar, G.N.D. University, Amritsar.

Based on WTTC estimates, tourism industry is all set to grow at a much faster rate. This is true about all countries, developed or developing, except South Asian countries including India.

India although endowed with a rich share of the essential ingredients attraction the fullest for tourists but we have failed to exploit our resources to potential. Lack of appropriate tourism planning and policies, ineffective marketing strategies, poor quality of tourism products and non-availability of trained professional managerial personnel are some of the factors which can be attributed to our poor performance at global level. Here lies the importance of manpower development.

The present paper, besides highlighting the above facts, emphasises on the growth of manpower development tourism institutions in India and benefits of trained manpower.

GLOBAL ECONOMIC SCENARIO

There is no denying the fact that at present the wind is flowing in favour of:

1. Liberalisation;

2. Globalisation;

3. Privatisation;

4. MNCs;

5. World Trade Organisation;

6. World Tourism Organisation;

7. Innovation;

8. Information technology;

9. Marketing revolution including E-Commerce, D-Commerce, M-Commerce and so forth.

All these are strong indicators of boundaryless economy. Earlier, the impression was given that such an economy may help various nations particularly the developing ones in improving their economy. In some quarters, there was a feeling that these new economic policies may enable new markets for goods and services from developed countries. All these claims and beliefs proved illusory. Boundaryless economy has neither helped the ailing economy of poor countries nor has it served the hidden agenda of G–7 which became G-8 after the induction of Russia.

Even after two decades of triple vaccine of liberalisation, privatisation and globalisation there has been no difference as far as the condition of poor countries or of poor living in such countries is concerned. As a matter of fact, their overall condition has worsened over these many years. As per United Nations Development Programme (UNDP) report, about 1.2 billion people in the developing countries live on less than one dollar a day and nearly 3.6 billion on less than two dollars a day. One billion people have no access to potable water and two billion are without basic sanitation facilities. Further, there are 325 million children and one billion adults in these countries who have never stepped inside a school. Moreover, about 163 million children under five are underweight and 11 million die every year from easily preventable causes. These figures speak themselves about the progress made by developing countries during a span of 20 years of economic reforms. Whether these are indices of development or abject poverty may be anybody's guess.

New economic policies have also failed to serve the purposes for developed nations too. It is evident from the fact that the International Monetary Fund (IMF) has been compelled to cut global growth forecast to 2.8 per cent from its previous estimate of 3.2 per cent and lower its 2002 global expansion outlook to 3.6 per cent from 3.8 per cent. The IMF source has pointed out that growth prospects of 12 nations of the Euro zone for 2002 have also been downgraded to a growth of 0.5 per cent as compared to an earlier prediction of 1.5 per cent. The prediction about USA is also not good.

Indian economy is also facing several problems. Fiscal deficit, unemployment and recession threats are continuously increasing while exports and imports have registered declining trends. Agriculture sector showed no progress while industrial growth in 2001 has been the lowest in the last eight years. Growth prospects for 2002 have been reduced to 5.2 in comparison to an earlier prediction of 6.4 per cent.

Thus, new economic policies (NEP) based on the IMF World Bank's Structural Programme (SAP) have not helped any country in bringing economic reforms. As a matter of fact, the economies of several developing countries have started deteriorating in post reform era.

ECONOMIC POTENTIAL OF TOURISM

Although present global economic scenario clearly signals tough challenges ahead but tourism has certainly emerged as a potential instrument for the economic development and growth of various countries.

According to a report recently released by World Travel and Tourism Council (WTTC), travel and tourism industry will play a key role in the rejuvenation of the world economy. Its research studies reveal that world travel and tourism business is likely to increase from $3 trillion in 1995 to $7.2 trillion in 2005. During the same period, tourism's share in consumer expenditure may increase from 11.4 per cent to 11.6 per cent, share in capital investment from 11.3 per cent to 11.8 per cent and jobs from 212 million to much more than 312 million. These figures indicate beyond doubt that tourism business is full of hopes and promises as far as economic prosperity at global level is concerned.

Indian estimates regarding tourism business are equally impressive. According to the CII tourism vision 2020 for India, the country's tourism exports currently account for $3 billion and the industry employs 10 million persons directly and another 10 million indirectly.

An additional one million visitors can generate Rs 4,300 crores. Every one million rupees invested in tourism sector can create 47.5 jobs or 12.6 jobs in manufacturing or 44.7 jobs in agriculture. The vision plan projects that by year 2020 one in every eight persons or an overall 50 million persons would be employed in travel and tourism economy. This sector would contribute 7 per cent of the GDP or Rs 10 lakh crores while the total tourist arrivals in the country would be 40 million or 4 per cent of world travel. The estimates seem to be on the higher side keeping in view the current comparative position of India at the global level.

India currently ranks 43rd in the world list of international tourist arrivals with 2.48 million tourists coming to the country out of more than 700 million tourists crossing international borders and spending close to 420 billion US dollars every year. Thus, our share is just 0.28 per cent of world travel.

Although our share in world travel and tourism is insignificant at present but it does not undermine the economic potential of tourism in the years to come. Moreover, present position can be improved if serious efforts are made to develop tourism in the country. The stage has reached where we will have to decide whether to progress or perish.

GLIMPSES OF NATIONAL TOURISM RESOURCES

India is endowed with a rich share of the essential ingredients of beauty attraction for tourists. We have an attractive variety of natural scenery ranging from snowcapped majestic Himalayas to the salubrious coasts of Kerala, from the golden desert of Rajasthan to the exciting jungles in our eastern states. Many moods of our climate coupled with an exotic reserve of wildlife add spice to it. Our unmatched cultural heritage and the mystique past embodied in exquisite archaeological and historical monuments; our festivals and fairs pulsating through the pomp and pageantry of rich tradition of performing arts; mind-boggling range of delectable cuisine; warm-hearted people are the rare assets not found in many parts of the world. Transportation and accommodation are also cheapest in India. In recent years, some steps such as development of select tourist areas and tourist spots, allowing hotel and tourism related industries to invite direct foreign investment upto 51 per cent, reduction in hotel expenditure tax, permission for importing 800 tourist cars, simplification of visa and foreigners registration rules, advertising and publicity about India as a destination in principal tourist markets, celebration of 'Visit India Year', introduction of action plan and announcement of new tourism policy have been taken up with a view to promote tourism and these are welcome measures.

X-RAYING TOURISM PERFORMANCE

In spite of reasonably adequate attractions and provision for other facilities for the tourists, we have failed to attract our due share of tourist clientele from abroad in particular. Various reasons account for this poor performance. Prominent among others are:

(i)   Lack of appropriate plans and policies;

(ii) Poor quality of tourist products;

(iii) Lack of dedicated efforts on our part to convince the potential tourists that the problem of terrorism pertaining only to some pockets of the country is effectively contained and that the law and order situation in general is as good as in any other country;

(iv) Little attention to human resources development; and

(v) Poor marketing strategies.

Major problems facing tourists are: frequent cancellation and inordinate delay particularly in internal flights; inefficient reservation system; unhygienic conditions in trains; poor sanitation facilities; and inadequacy of surface transport for various categories of tourists. Further, whether one travels by road or by rail, hygienic and wholesome food is difficult to come by. In recent years, travel by Air India/ Indian Airlines has become more risky. These are such irritants that can be taken care of with a little effort and fore-planning but their persistence definitely erodes the credibility of our tourist industry.

MANPOWER DEVELOPMENT – A FORMIDABLE REMEDY

A lot has been said about the above problems but very little about their solution. Of late, some efforts have been made on the fronts of planning, improving quality of tourist products and curbing terrorism. However, due attention has not been paid to manpower development/ tourism education/ hotel management education. Tourism and hotel management education is, of course, of vital importance in developing right kind of manpower which in turn can make better planning and bring required professionalism to tourism and hotel industry.

Tourism Management Education

Till now no worthwhile efforts have been made either by the Ministry of Human Resource Development or the Ministry of

Tourism or even by the UGC to promote tourism education. Virtually no thought was given to tourism education till 1983 when an Indian Institute of Tourism and Travel Management (IITTM) was established to act as nodal agency for spreading tourism education, holding seminars and conferences and running periodical courses related to tour and travel business. IITTM, has now decided to start a postgraduate degree course on tourism. The story could have been different had it been run on the pattern of Indian Institute of Management at Calcutta or Ahmedabad or Bangalore.

A modest breakthrough in this regard was made by Kurukshetra University in July 1990 when it introduced two courses, i.e. Master of Tourism Management (MTM), a two year (4-semesters) programme and Postgraduate Diploma in Destination Management (PGDDM), a one year (2-semesters) programme. Led by Kurukshetra University, about 10 more universities (Indore August 1991, Jodhpur – October 1991, Shimla, 1992, Pondicherry – January 1992, Aligarh – January 1992, Aurangabad – February 1992, H.N.B. Garhwal, Anantpur, Managalore, Shillong and Bangalore – April 1992) have also started Master of Tourism Administration (MTA) courses. Recently some more universities, namely Agra University, Jiwaji University, Gwalior, Bundelkhand University, Jhansi University, Burdwan University (WB), etc. have also launched this tourism education programme. About 8,00 students are receiving formal tourism education in these institutions.

It is surprising that out of 239 universities, deemed universities, institutes of national importance, only about 15 institutions are providing tourism education at postgraduation level. Further, out of 11,534 colleges about 100 colleges at the initiative of UGC are running tourism as vocational course at graduation level. About 4,000 students are admitted by these colleges every year. Thus, in all, less than 5,000 graduates are available against more than 26,000 trained personnel required by tourism industry every year. The supply against demand is indeed low. All these figures reflect a gloomy picture of tourism education. The Ministries of Human Resources Development and Tourism as well as UGC should give serious thought towards the promotion of tourism education in the country so that adequate trained manpower is made available to tourism industry.

A few suggestions are made for the healthy growth of tourism education. These are:

(i) **Financial Aid:** Institutions imparting tourism education must receive liberal financial help from the Ministry of Human Resource Development, the Ministry of Tourism and the UGC at least during the first five years. Funds are essential for creating necessary infrastructure and developing faculty in addition to carrying out research, holding seminars and conferences and arranging workshops.

(ii) **Link between Educational Institutions and Tourism Undertakings:** Syllabi for tourism education must meet the requirements of tourism undertakings. Similarly, tourism undertakings should educate the students of tourism about job training and placement opportunities. Thus, tourism industry shall not have to face the shortage of right kind of manpower while the students shall have ample opportunities for getting jobs. For the balanced growth of tourism education in relation to the growth of tourism industry, there is need for better understanding and rapport between the educational institutions and tourism undertakings.

The courses prepared by Kurukshetra University in consultation with nodal agency, the Ministry of Tourism, the leading tour and travel agencies and experts in this field are capable of meeting the growing requirements of various organisations such as travel agencies, tour operators, hoteliers, tourism corporations, national parks, sanctuaries, zoos, heritage centres, embassies, railways, airlines and tourism education institutions. Needless to say that the syllabi must be revised from time to time as per requirements of the industry.

(iii) *PGDDM/ MTM/ MTA as Desirable Qualification:* Tourism undertakings whether in the public sector or private sector may at least mention PGDDM/ MTM/ MTA as desirable qualifications while sending advertisement for various jobs at operational and middle managerial level respectively. This will give a psychological advantage and boost the morale of those pursuing tourism education.

(iv) *Special Column for Tourism Jobs in Classified Advertisement:* Newspapers and journals carrying advertisements related to tourism undertakings should provide special column to such advertisements. This, in addition to signifying the jobs for persons with special educational background, shall also highlight the status of tourism industry which has emerged as the single largest foreign exchange earning industry in addition to providing employment to about 20 million workers in the country.

Hotel Management Education

Our hotel industry is also ill equipped as far as varied requirements of trained manpower by the industry is concerned. At present, there are about 17 institutes at lower middle management level and equal number of institutes at craft level. Both types of institutions are developing a committed and efficient human resource at all levels. Perhaps, there can be no industry other than tourism where we need human resource manpower development most, at present.

BENEFITS OF MANPOWER DEVELOPMENT

Manpower development is largely a matter of good education, training and of attempting to place people in the right jobs so that they can be more productive. When employees are properly developed the employee, the undertaking, and the society all benefit.

The benefits that employees may receive from proper development are: linear 1- Higher pay; 2 – Job satisfaction; 3 – Opportunity for promotion; and 4 – A change to develop new skills.

The undertakings receive as benefit a "fair day's work for fair day's pay". This in turn allows the undertaking to stay competitive so that it can profitably sell its goods or services. Profitable operations of the business assure the investors a fair return on their investment and keep the undertaking in business, which gives the employee job security.

The benefit to society is greater productivity or improved productivity or both. The improved or increased productivity raises the nation's standard of living and keeps it competitive in the world market.

Trained manpower ensures better tourism planning, effective marketing and optimal use of existing resources. Leading institutes are admitting almost equal number of students, i.e. about 2,000 students each year. The requirement of the hotel industry is many times more than the annual intake of hotel education institutions. This is particularly true at craft level and upper middle management level. There is no hotel management education institute in India providing postgraduate degree in hotel management. It amply proves the importance being given to hotel management education in India.

CONCLUSION

The above discussion leads us to believe that there is no dearth of basic resources and infrastructure to develop tourism on sound footings. However, we have so far clearly failed to tap all these resources and consequently to develop tourism to our potential. The single factor which can be attributed to this sorry state of affairs is utter negligence of human resources development (HRD) or manpower development. Be it on the front of tourism planning or developing appropriate tourists resorts or selling India abroad or handling of air, rail and road transports or providing hospitality or curbing terrorism and violence, we are found wanting.

Now, we cannot afford to let our resources go untapped or remain under-utilised. The appropriate and effective utilisation of resources is must and it can be ensured by increase in tourist arrivals and tourism earnings. Thus, manpower development means tourism development and that is what we want at present.

REFERENCES

Statistics used in this paper have been compiled from various publications of WTO, IATO, etc.

Extracts have been taken from author's earlier publications such as "Tourism Education" 'HRD' – A Way to Develop Tourism' Appeared in National and International Journals.

Recent Statistical Data published by IMF and World Bank sources.